The Common Teachings of Four Mystical Traditions

JESUS
BUDDHA
KRISHNA
LAO TZU

The Parallel Sayings

The Common Teachings of Four Mystical Traditions

JESUS
BUDDHA
KRISHNA
LAO TZU

The Parallel Sayings

Edited and with an introduction by

RICHARD HOOPER

SANCTUARY PUBLICATIONS

Jesus, Buddha, Krishna and Lao Tzu: The Parallel Sayings

Cover and book design: Jane Perini, Thunder Mountain Design & Communications
Production assistant: Atara Heiss

The graphic on page 65 is a revelation of Terton Migyur Dorje (17th Century, Tibet). It is considered sacred in the Vajrayana Buddhist tradition and is known as "Liberation Upon Sight."

Photograph of Mahatma Gandhi used with the friendly permission of
www.yogaindailylife.org

Photographs on pages 26, 75, 86, 115, 152 by Sharon Hooper, www.VisionJourneys.com

Photographs on pages 70, 162, 165 courtesy of Wib Middleton,
Thunder Mountain Design & Communications

Published by Sanctuary Publications, Inc., P.O. Box 20697, Sedona, AZ 86341

ISBN 9780978533496
LCCN 2007903204

Dedicated to the memory of

Eknath Easwaran,

a true wise man from the East

CONTENTS

"You must make the effort
yourself. The masters
only point the way."

– *The Buddha*, The Dhammapada

INTRODUCTION

"If the doors of perception were cleansed,
everything would appear to man as it is, infinite.
For man has closed himself up, till he sees all things
through narrow chinks of his cavern."

– *William Blake,* The Marriage of Heaven and Hell

The Mystical Imperative

The story goes that, after his enlightenment, Siddhartha Gautama—the historical Buddha— was walking down the road when he met a fellow traveler. The other man perceived a great radiance emanating from Siddhartha, so instead of asking, "Who are you, he asked, "Are you a god or a divine being? "No," answered the Buddha. "Are you a shaman or a sorcerer?" "No," answered the Buddha. "Are you a man?" Again the Buddha answered, "No." "Well, then," the man said, "what are you?" The Buddha answered, "I am awake." And, indeed, this is what "Buddha" means: one who is awakened.

According to the Gospels of the New Testament, much the same thing happened in the case of Jesus. Siddhartha was tempted by Mara, the Evil One, and when he was victorious over all temptation, he "woke up." The story of Jesus' temptation in the wilderness is almost a carbon copy of the Buddha legend. Jesus, like the Buddha, was victorious over all the temptations of "Satan," and in the moment of his victory, he was utterly changed. As he walked by the seashore, fishermen saw his radiance, dropped their nets and followed him. As he walked through pastures and fields, farmers let go of their plows and followed him. As with the

Buddha, everyone who met Jesus knew he was no ordinary man. What made these two men special? For one thing, they both had profound wisdom. But their wisdom was unlike others because it came, not from intellectual reasoning, but from direct awareness of the Absolute. Jesus and the Buddha were mystics. Their teachings carried the weight of authority because they came from the source of Being itself. Their personal wisdom was not the result of religious belief or faith, but came from a place of *gnosis*—knowledge.

A century ago William James in *The Varieties of Religious Experience* observed, "…mystical states seem to those who experience them to be states of knowledge. They are states of sight into depths of truth unplumbed by the discursive intellect…and as a rule they carry with them a curious sense of authority for aftertime."[1]

The Gospel stories about Jesus, for instance, claim that those who heard him were amazed that he spoke with "authority," not like the priests or the other teachers of his day. Had Jesus not had charisma, wisdom, and *knowledge*, it is highly doubtful anyone would have remembered his words.

People who met the Buddha knew immediately that he had had some profound experience, and that the experience had altogether altered him. Like Jesus, when the Buddha spoke, people listened because they recognized his words as coming from somewhere other than the intellectual mind. They seemed to come from the Source of understanding itself.

I first read the words of Krishna in the *Bagavad Gita* some forty years ago. At the time, I was still very much a

committed and believing Christian—heading to seminary after college. Yet I found myself fascinated with Krishna's words in the same way that I was by Jesus. Those words didn't seem to agree with Christian dogmas but, for me, they had the ring of truth. When I later read the teachings attributed to Lao Tzu in the *Tao Te Ching*, I had the very same reaction.

Even though these teachers represent four different world religions, I believe their teachings have a great deal in common. Could it be that their teachings represent four slightly different paths to the same destination? Each of these masters claimed that their teachings came from personal experience of ultimate reality, so we might expect their teachings to be similar. Certainly their teachings carry the weight of authority—in our day, as well as theirs.

If the words of certain teachers move us, and if we were to examine our thoughts while reading them, what often strikes us most is not that these teachers are telling us something new, but that they are reminding us of something we already knew but, perhaps, had forgotten! It is as if we had always known these truths at some deep level, so we respond with, "Aha!" "Yes, of course! I knew that all along!" These teachers reveal the truth that has always been within us.

But the teachings that come from those in touch with the Absolute still have limitations. Mystical insight has the nature of ineffability. Direct awareness of Ultimate Reality—

[1] William James, The Varieties of Religious Experience, Collier Macmillan, New York, 1961, p. 300.

and for our purposes we will assume that's what it is—can never be adequately communicated in words. James says of the mystical experience, "The subject of it immediately says that it defies expression, that no adequate report of its contents can be given in words."[2] The most any mystic can do is to convey approximations of his or her experience. Teaching therefore, often takes the form of negation: "Not this, not that."

Certainly history has had many mystics who didn't try to communicate their understanding to others. Others have tried and failed. In the case of Jesus, for instance, the canonical Gospels make it clear that even his closest disciples didn't "get it" much of the time. Teachers may do their very best to convey mystical insight using parables, dialectic, symbolism and other forms of wisdom teaching, but in the end, the words will always fall short of the reality. So the words of even the greatest teachers are, at best, no more than road signs on the path to understanding. They are, more often than not, cautionary: Yield; Watch for falling rocks; Slow down, you're going the wrong way.

Every true teacher knows that all those who follow must seek enlightenment through their own personal efforts, in their own individual way. The teacher can give advice, prescribe methodology, and steer the student away from unproductive paths, but in the end—everyone is on their own.

And this is the limitation of organized religion as well. Once the teacher is gone, all bets are off. Religious devotees have a tendency to codify their teachers' wisdom, but in doing so they turn living truth into a pale transparency of itself. The moment anyone's teachings become packaged for mass

consumption, the essence of those teachings will become lost to one degree or another.

Official canons, while important, can often short circuit the effectiveness of a spiritual path, and even create deception. Certainly this happens when the teacher is elevated to divine status and worshipped as Truth itself. This is why Buddhists say such things as, "Do not seek the Buddha, seek what the Buddha sought," or, "If you meet the Buddha on the road, kill him!"

Jesus told his followers that the answer was within *themselves*: "If those who lead you say the Kingdom of heaven is in the sky, then the birds of the sky will get there before you do. If they say it is in the sea, then the fish will beat you there. Rather, the kingdom is within you…"[3] Every teaching, every word—no matter how profound—is only a guidepost along the way. Every seeker is a pilgrim, and every pilgrim travels alone.

The Value and Limitation of Words

Nevertheless, I think teachings are important. They guide us and inspire us, and they represent humanity's common effort to seek ultimate knowledge. Ultimately—and I think most teachers would agree—the teachings are more important than the teacher. That's important to mention here because *the words attributed to Jesus, Krishna, the Buddha and Lao Tzu did not necessarily originate with those men.*

[2] Ibid, pp. 299-300.
[3] The Gospel of Thomas 3a.

Of the four, only Jesus and the Buddha are considered to be historical figures. As an avatar, Krishna (Hinduism considers the Buddha and Jesus to have been avatars as well) is the mythical incarnation of Ishvara—a personal deity who, in turn, is an emanation of Brahman, the ultimate Godhead. And while there is a "history" of the Chinese sage, Lao Tzu— a name which simply means "old master"—most scholars do not take it seriously, and believe the Tao Te Ching was written anonymously.

In fact, all the texts that we will consider here were written anonymously. The Gospels, for instance, have no author's names attached. These works were simply attributed to Matthew, Mark, Luke and John by Christians at a later date. In the case of Siddhartha Gautama, the historical Buddha, none of his actual words remain. Siddhartha spoke Ardhamagadhi, and none of his sayings are preserved in that form. All that remains are translations of the earliest Buddhist canons; and since Buddhism, like Christianity, began as an oral tradition, the Buddha's actual words are lost to us.

We know somewhat more about the words of the historical Jesus, but not nearly as much as most Christians think. Jesus and his original followers spoke Aramaic, (the New Testament was written entirely in Greek by Greek-speaking Christians) and they left no writings at all. Many of the words attributed to Jesus were actually the words of the anonymous authors who, unlike Jesus, were Christians. Neither were any of these men eye-witnesses to the life and teachings of Jesus. Jesus' own disciples left no writings, and the earliest narrative Gospel (*The Gospel of Mark*) was written no earlier

than 70 C.E., about forty years after Jesus was killed. It was written from Rome by someone who knew very little about the actual life of Jesus.

John and Matthew's Gospels were written near the end of the first century, and the *Gospel of Luke* may have been composed as late as 120 C.E. Ancient mythologists (and that includes Hindus, Buddhists and Taoists) thought nothing of putting their own words into their teachers' mouths, and in the case of Jesus, they made him a Christian retrospectively. The historical Jesus did not believe himself to be the Messiah, or son of God, as is born out by the earliest "source" gospels.[4]

Certain groups of New Testament scholars, such as the Jesus Seminar, suggest that as few as eighteen percent of all the words attributed to Jesus in the canonical Gospels actually came from him, and even these are probably not in their original form. In the case of the apocryphal and Gnostic Gospels, the problem is even more pronounced.

In spite of all this, those who invented the words attributed to Jesus, Krishna, the Buddha and Lao Tzu, believed that they were writing *in the spirit* of these great teachers—which is to say, the anonymous authors of each text believed that their teacher would have said these words had he been given the opportunity.

The ancient mythologists were anything but literalists, believing that the words they put in their teacher's mouth were *true*, even if they weren't *historical*. And perhaps this is a good guide for the reader as well. If the words in this book have the ring of truth, then it probably doesn't matter *who* originally said or wrote them.

Wise Men from the East

I have wanted to present a comparison of Jesus' teachings with those of the Eastern masters for a long time—in fact ever since I was introduced to Eastern philosophy at college. As a young man headed to seminary after college, I wanted to know what the teachers of other religions had to say, so I took a major in Eastern and Western philosophy. Though

I didn't know it at the time, I had set myself on a path that would eventually lead right out the back door of the Church. Yet my disagreements with "orthodox" Christianity began as a child.

I recall one night—I think I was thirteen years of age—when the pastor of our church was talking to our youth group. He was telling us that anyone who did not believe in Jesus would not go to heaven, intimating that they would go to that *other* place instead. This statement shocked me.

I raised my hand and then asked the pastor, "Do you mean to say that even someone living in a far away place like India, who has never even heard of Jesus, will go to hell because they don't believe in him?" To my utter amazement, the pastor answered in the affirmative.

I couldn't believe my ears. I knew I was just a kid, but I thought that this was the dumbest thing I ever heard. I respected the pastor and believed that he must be in contact with truth, but in this case I knew in my heart that he was wrong. Since I believed in Jesus, I also believed in his Father—who he described as a God of love and compassion. So I chose to believe Jesus rather than my pastor because I could not accept that a loving God would be unfair and send people to hell for no good reason.

Many people who are interested in Eastern philosophy have probably had similar experiences while growing up in the

---

[4] Two source Gospels, the Gospel known as "Q", aka the *Synoptic Sayings Source*, and parts of *The Gospel of Thomas* were written as early as 50 C.E., and show no evidence of "Christian" teachings.

Christian Church. Their own personal disconnects may have caused them to start questioning the dogmas of the Church, and whether Christianity really reflects the teachings of Jesus. Many people may sense that the religion *about* Jesus is quite different than the religion *of* Jesus.

Such criticisms of Christianity are hardly new. Ever since the Enlightenment, thoughtful Christians have been asking whether the teachings of the Church have any real relationship to the man upon whom the Church was supposedly founded. In 1884, Leo Tolstoy published a book entitled *My Religion*, and his words probably reflect the views of many former Christians:

> From my childhood, from the time I first began to read the New Testament, I was touched most of all by that portion of the doctrine of Jesus which inculcates love, humility, self-denial, and the duty of returning good for evil. This, to me, has always been the substance of Christianity; my heart recognized its truth in spite of skepticism and despair, and for this reason I submitted to a religion professed by a multitude of toilers, who find in it the solution of life—the religion taught by the Orthodox Church. But in making my submission to the Church, I soon saw that I should not find in its creed the confirmation of the essence of Christianity; what was to me essential seemed to be in the dogma of the Church merely an accessory. What was to me the most important teachings of Jesus was not so regarded by the Church... What I found most repulsive in the doctrine of the Church was the strangeness of its dogmas and the approval, nay, the support, which it gave to persecutions, to the death penalty, to wars stirred up by the intolerance common to all sects; but my faith was chiefly shattered by the indifference of the Church to what seemed to me essential in the teachings of Jesus...[5]

Tolstoy's disconnect with the Church began to form in his mind even as a child. This is not surprising since children can be quite sensitive to hypocrisy. Tolstoy speaks for many of us who have left the Church, but have *not* turned away from Jesus. While the Church may have been found wanting, Jesus still speaks to the ages.

As the age of unbelief dawned in the West, a wave of exotic religious ideas from Eastern religions began to wash up on the shores of Europe and America, giving Christians and former Christians the chance to compare the teachings of Jesus with the teachings of Eastern religions—especially Hinduism.

Theosophy became a major Western philosophical movement during the nineteenth century, and many, if not most, of its ideas were drawn from Hinduism. Karma, reincarnation and the study of the chakras of the human body all came to the West via India during the nineteenth century. The translation of Hinduism's most sacred text, *The Bagavad Gita* (The Lords Song) into English during that century even influenced such great authors as Emerson and Thoreau.

---

[5] Count Lyof N. Tolstoy, My Religion, London, Walter Scott Publishing, pp. 2-3.

A second wave of Hinduism washed ashore when Swami Vivekananda established the Vedanta Society in New York in 1894, and Paramahansa Yogananda founded a yoga institute in Los Angeles in 1925 (which would later become the Self-Realization Fellowship.) The teachings of Shankara and Ramakrishna, the Yoga Aphorisms of Patanjali, all became established—albeit in a small way—in Western culture.

The path was thus prepared for yet another invasion of holy men from the East beginning in the 1960s. The Maharishi Mahesh Yogi popularized the practice of meditation, and counted as his early disciples such entertainment luminaries as the Beatles, Clint Eastwood, Mia Farrow and Merv Griffin. Swami Satchidananda gave the invocation at the Woodstock Festival in 1969. Swami Muktananda, Krishnamurti, Sri Chinmoy, Satya Sai Baba, Bhagwan Shree Rajneesh, Eknath Easwaran and a host of other Hindu teachers all had tremendous influence on the Counter Culture movement of the 1960s and '70s.

Arriving during this same time period, in much smaller numbers, were the missionaries of Buddhism. The great Rinzai master Soyen Shaku introduced Zen Buddhism to America in 1893. The Zen authors, D.T. Suzuki and Shunryu Suzuki Roshi provided the foundation of Zen thought for thousands of readers during the twentieth century. The Tibetan Buddhist lama, Chogyam Trungpa Rinpoche, along with many other lamas, popularized Tibetan Buddhism in the United States during the second half of the twentieth century. It would be hard to find anyone in the West today who has not at least heard of the Dalai Lama—the world's foremost ambassador of good will. The West has also produced its own "Eastern" teachers: Alan Watts, Ram Dass, Richard Baker Roshi and scores of others.

Taoism, a Chinese philosophy that dates back thousands of years, did not send its missionaries to the West, but its influence has been felt nonetheless. Most Westerners are primarily familiar with ancient Taoism through two books: The *Tao Te Ching* and the *Tao of Chuang Tzu*. But Taoist principles are also found in the oracle, the I Ching (The Book of Change), in the practice of Tai Chi Chuan, in acupuncture and in Chinese medicine. The symbol of the Tao—the yin/yang—can be seen virtually everywhere in the United States, and with "the Force" of Star Wars fame, movie producer George Lucas popularized the science fiction version of Tao.

If the old religions of Western culture have failed to provide meaning for many people today, can Eastern religions do any better? Only time will tell. To date it seems that their primary influence has not been in the form of establishing outposts, but in influencing non-traditional movements which have repackaged Eastern philosophy to fit a different time, a different land, and a different culture. Certainly the New Age movement is chief among such repackaging centers, and has all but become a religion in itself.

As the New Age movement has evolved (some would say, devolved) since the 1970s, much of it has often wandered off into realms of new mythologies, superstition and the occult. In spite of this rather discouraging trend, many "new age" principles are firmly founded on the basic insights of Eastern philosophy. This new religious culture in the West has made its own contributions as well. While classic religious texts

produced by the religions of the East are little read, most Hindu, Buddhist and Taoist teachings in the West today come from Western authors who, while being directly influenced by Eastern religions, have reformulated ancient truths for modern times and Western sensibilities. Even those books written by Buddhist monks, Tibetan lamas and Indian gurus are written to appeal to the modern—Western—reader. It would seem that in every age, that which is old must be made new again.

Of course, few spiritual insights are ever *really* new. The anonymous author who called himself "the Preacher" addressed this in the Biblical book known as *Ecclesiastes*:

> What has been is what will be, and what has been done is what will be done; and there is nothing new under the sun. Is there a thing of which it is said, "See, this is new?" It has been already, in the ages before us. There is no remembrance of former things, nor will there be any remembrance of later things yet to happen among those who come after.[6]

The Preacher was a pessimist perhaps, but he had a point. Science has the potential to change our worldview, but there really isn't anything new under the sun when it concerns religion, philosophy and metaphysics. Every insight has been revealed before by someone, somewhere. And while it is often helpful to reformulate age old teachings, it is also useful to reread the classic texts of religion which are themselves the product of numerous sages over great spans of time. For some readers, the wisdom of the ages makes the most sense coming in the words of the original masters, hence this book.

East Meets West

When comparing the insights of different teachers we find either similarities or dissimilarities, or a combination of both. Dissimilarity is to be expected and is easily explainable: different teacher, different religion and culture, and different periods of time.

Similarities, on the other hand, often do call out for an explanation. How is it that two teachers who lived during different eras, in countries widely separated, and whose religions and cultures were quite different, make almost identical statements about spirituality and the meaning of life? Immediately the historian and the theologian will suspect a causal link. One philosophy or religion must have influenced another. More often than not, these suspicions turn out to be correct.

There is no question that Hinduism was the foundation for Buddhism. Siddhartha Gautama was born in India, and Buddhism in the beginning was considered just another Hindu sect. For the first two hundred and fifty years of its existence, Buddhism's influence was strictly limited to the borders of India. By the time of its first missionary success in Ceylon, around 240 CE, Buddhism had already broken down into a number of sects. Each sect produced new literature, and the words of those texts were attributed to the historical Buddha.

Buddhism and Hinduism certainly had some influence on Greek philosophy, and Greek philosophy, in turn, influenced

_____

[6] Ecclesiastes 1:8-11.

first century Judaism, early orthodox Christianity and Gnosticism. But Buddhism and Hinduism may have had a more direct influence on Gnostic Christianity.

More than thirty years ago, Elaine Pagels in her seminal study, *The Gnostic Gospels*, asked whether Gnostic Christianity might have been directly influenced by these two Eastern religions:

> Could Hindu or Buddhist traditions have influenced Gnosticism? The British scholar of Buddhism, Edward Conze, suggests that it had. He points out that "Buddhists were in contact with the Thomas Christians (that is, Christians who knew and used such writings as the Gospel of Thomas) in South India." Trade routes between the Greco-Roman world and the Far East were opening up at the time when Gnosticism flourished (A.D. 80—200); for generations, Buddhist missionaries had been proselytizing in Alexandria. We note, too, that Hippolytus, who was a Greek speaking Christian in Rome (c. 225), knows of Indian Brahmins—and includes their tradition among the sources of heresy...Could the title of the *Gospel of Thomas*—named for the disciple who, tradition tells us, went to India—suggest the influence of Indian tradition? These hints indicate the possibility, yet our evidence is not conclusive. Since parallel traditions may emerge in different cultures at different times, such ideas could have developed in both places independently.[7]

Only time will tell if scholars can tease out more evidence of direct influence. But while there are shreds of evidence

suggesting a possible connection between Hinduism and Buddhism and Christian Gnosticism, there is not even a hint of evidence that Jesus himself was influenced by either of these two Eastern religions.

Was Jesus influenced by Hindus or Buddhists?

Jesus was, of course, a Jew, but since he challenged the priesthood of the Temple, as well as many of the norms, customs and laws of Judaism, we naturally wonder if he was influenced by philosophies and religions other than Judaism. During the time of Jesus, Judea/Palestine was rife with sectarian movements, as well as religious philosophies which had their roots in the Gentile world. So Jesus may have been influenced by any combination of those influences.

Because John the Baptist plays such an important role in the canonical Gospels, scholars have long taken it for granted that Jesus had been John's disciple prior to the beginning of his own ministry. John, however, was a messianic and apocalyptic preacher who believed the end of the world was at hand. For John, repentance was the necessary response to the coming Kingdom of God, since only the righteous would be saved.

Jesus, on the other hand, did not believe the world was about to end[8], but taught that the Kingdom of God was here

---

[7] Elaine Pagels, *The Gnostic Gospels*, New York, Vantage Press, 1989, p. xxi.
[8] The Church has always taught otherwise, but recent work on the source Gospels of "Q" and the first layer of tradition in the *Gospel of Thomas* show that Jesus was not an apocalyptic preacher like John.

and now. While John called for repentance and a change of behavior, Jesus taught that people just needed to perceive reality with new eyes. If they could alter their perception, Jesus knew, they would see that God was everywhere, most especially within themselves.

If Jesus had been a disciple of John, then the two men may have split over disagreements on such issues. In that event, they would have been teachers in competition with one another. But there is also the possibility that Jesus was never personally associated with John at all, and that the Baptist tradition was fused with the Jesus tradition after the Baptists joined the Jesus movement when John was beheaded by King Herod. It is equally possible that Baptists (who were messianists) had no association with the Jesus people either, but joined Paul's Messianist (Christian) movement years after the death of Jesus. In this event, the Christian authors of the Gospels—who wrote much later still—combined the two traditions in their mythological stories about Jesus and John.

Over the years, a host of people outside the Christian academic community have suggested that Jesus may have been an Essene, or that John was an Essene, or both. But there is no real evidence to suggest such a connection. There are some similarities between the Essenes and John, but that does not hold true for Jesus. Jesus' teachings were incompatible with those of the Essenes—or those sectaries of Qumran that people assume were Essenes.

There is evidence for yet another possibility: the canonical Gospels often referred to Jesus as "the Nazarene." The Church—and most scholars as well—have always claimed that the title, Nazarene, indicated that Jesus had come from the town of Nazareth in Galilee. But there are some scholars who now contest this assumption and suggest that there was an actual Jewish mystical sect known as the Nazarenes, and it is even possible that Jesus was the leader of this sect.

All of this is guesswork at best. We actually know almost nothing about Jesus' early influences. In the earliest narrative Gospel, *Mark*, Jesus just suddenly appears on the scene in the company of John the Baptist. Since the author of this Gospel was a Greek-speaking Gentile, probably writing from Rome some forty years after the death of Jesus, he apparently felt no need to invent an early life of Jesus. All that mattered to him was what Jesus did during the single year of his ministry.

Neither was the author of John's Gospel—written much later—compelled to invent an early history of Jesus. But the authors of *Matthew* and *Luke*, writing near the end of the first century, wanted to tie Jesus to Israel's prophetic history. To do this, they had to create fictional stories based on Biblical prophecy. Those stories, like Luke's story of Jesus being presented at the Temple at age twelve, are myths, not history.

The general public, unfortunately, does not read the work of Biblical scholars, so the average reader has the tendency to interpret the Bible as if it were literal history. As a consequence, various people outside academia during the nineteenth century began speculating about what Jesus might have been doing during all those "missing" years (between the ages of twelve and thirty) prior to beginning his public ministry. Surely he hadn't gained all his wisdom from Judaism; he must have traveled to far away places like India and Tibet where he studied with Hindu gurus and Buddhist lamas.

Such speculation, initially, was the result of various English and American critics of orthodox Christianity who had begun to adopt Eastern philosophy for the first time as a result of the first wave of Indian gurus coming to the West during the nineteenth century. Strongly influenced by Hinduism, new American movements such as the Theosophical Society, founded by Helena Petrovna Blavatsky, in New York in 1875, began considering the possibility of a connection between Jesus and Hinduism.

Anne Besant took up the cause when Madame Blavatsky died, and the Society spawned spin-offs like the "I Am" movement founded by Guy Warren Ballard, later taken to new heights by Mark and Elizabeth Claire Prophet, who founded Summit Lighthouse. This organization, along with later movements such as the Self Realization Fellowship founded by Paramahansa Yogananda, all had a vested interest in establishing a connection between Jesus, Hinduism and Buddhism.

Such organizations became easy prey for charlatans who manufactured fictional stories about Jesus having traveled to India and Tibet. The best known of these stories was told by Nicholas Notovitch—a Russian Jew who converted to Greek Orthodoxy. In 1887 Notovitch wrote a book titled the *Unknown Life of Jesus Christ*, in which he included a legend about a man known as Saint Issa. As the story unfolds, it turns out that Saint Issa was really Jesus, and this Jesus

had gone to Tibet to study with Buddhist lamas—or so Notovitch claimed.

Shortly after Notovitch published his book, the great Orientalist, Max Muller, along with other scholars of his day, took it upon themselves to debunk Notovitch's story and expose it as a hoax—which indeed it turned out to be. For those who are interested in this drama, I have included an analysis of the whole affair in an appendix at the back of this book.

Suffice it to say that if Notovitch had known the first thing about Buddhist history, he would not have invented his Saint Issa hoax. Jesus could not have studied with Tibetan Buddhist lamas for the very simple reason that Buddhism didn't reach Tibet until *seven centuries* after Jesus' death! Had Jesus gone to Tibet, he would have discovered, not Buddhists, but shamans and practitioners of Bon, the indigenous religion of Tibet—which worshiped a pantheon of spirits, and practiced animal—and sometimes human—sacrifice.

Had Jesus actually gained his wisdom from Eastern gurus, he would be a much less imposing historical and religious figure. It is Jesus' uniqueness from all other teachers that has always made him important. Jesus, while being a mystic, was not a quietist, as the Buddha and most mystics are. He was a social revolutionary as well as a spiritual one. He stood up to the hypocrisy of those who publicly made a display of their religion, and he challenged the social order—the inequities of Jewish society.

This book, however, is about similarities, not differences. And Jesus' similarities to other great religious figures, like his social criticism, probably came naturally—not as a result of being indoctrinated by wise men from the East. Consider this: if Jesus was an enlightened being—which I like to think he was—would he not have taught many of the same things that Krishna, the Buddha, and Lao Tzu did? If Jesus tapped into the Source of Being itself, how could his teachings not have similarities to the teachings of other enlightened beings?

What impresses me the most about Jesus as a person who "woke up", is that he tried to explain his mystical insights to people who didn't have the slightest idea of what he was talking about. The Buddha was fortunate enough to "wake up" in India—the most mystically oriented culture on Earth. When people met him after his enlightenment they would say, "Congratulations, we knew you could do it!" When Jesus woke up in first century Palestine, he must have looked around at his situation and thought, "uh oh."

Certainly Jesus could have kept his new mystical understanding of reality to himself. Had he done so—had he just enjoyed his private bliss in the Kingdom of God—he might have lived to a ripe old age, and died a peaceful death like the historical Buddha. But Jesus was passionate, and felt compelled to share his wisdom with as many other people as he could reach. This meant that he had no choice but to try to explain himself within the doctrinal and social confines of a religious culture that was completely unfamiliar with, and mostly antagonistic to, mystical insights about reality.

While Siddhartha Gautama was supported by a community of mystics, many of those Jesus talked to thought he was either crazy, or blasphemous, or both. His own family rejected him and thought him demented. Most of Jesus' disciples, while obviously charmed by his charisma, often didn't understand what he was talking about. In the end, one of them betrayed him, another denied him, and the rest deserted him in his greatest hour of need.

Whatever Jesus' influences were, his teachings are often startlingly similar to those of the Eastern masters. Marcus Borg is one Jesus scholar today who sees those similarities clearly. In his book, *Jesus and Buddha—the Parallel Sayings*, Borg has this to say:

> ...the cumulative product of my thinking and experience is the conclusion that Jesus and the

Buddha are the two most remarkable religious figures who have ever lived. Moreover, there are striking similarities between them. I have sometimes said that if the Buddha and Jesus were to meet, neither would try to convert the other—not because they would regard such an effort as hopeless, but because they would recognize one another.

...Jesus and the Buddha were teachers of wisdom. Wisdom is more than ethics, even though it includes ethical teaching. The "more" consists of funda-mental ways of seeing and being. Wisdom is not just about moral behavior, but about the "center." The place from which moral perception and moral behavior flow.

Jesus and Buddha were teachers of a world-subverting wisdom that undermined and challenged conventional ways of seeing and being in their time and in every time. Their subversive wisdom was also an alternative wisdom: they taught a way or path of transformation.[9]

Another Christian who was aware of this East/West connec-tion was the great Catholic monk and mystic, Thomas Merton. Much of his life was dedicated to finding the similar-ities between Western and Eastern monasticism and mysti-cism. He traveled extensively in Asian lands, had a special affinity for Buddhism, especially Zen, and wrote *Zen and the Birds of Appetite*. In his final work, *The Asian Journal*, Merton expressed his love for Eastern religions and expounded on the importance of the sacred Hindu text, The *Bagavad Gita*.

As for the ancient teachings of Taoism, Merton wrote his own translation of *The Way of Chuang Tzu*.

There have also been many Hindu and Buddhist teachers who have approached the subject of commonality between Jesus' teachings and their own. One such contemporary teacher is the Vietnamese Buddhist monk, Thich Nhat Hanh, who wrote *Living Buddha, Living Christ, and Going Home: Jesus and Buddha as Brothers*. It is worth noting that the Introduction to *Living Buddha, Living Christ* was written by Elaine Pagels, and the Foreword by the Catholic monk, Brother David Steindl-Rast.

One Reality or Two?

While Christianity has its failings, were it not for that religion, virtually none of Jesus' teachings would have survived. The world would never have heard of him, because the early Jesus movement built around his teachings disappeared after 70 C.E. when Jerusalem was destroyed by the Romans, and the Jews were forced into exile in the first great Diaspora. Ironically, it was the religion *about* Jesus which preserved the religion *of* Jesus.

Jesus was not a Christian, however. Contemporary New Testament scholars argue that Jesus never identified himself with God, nor did he think of himself as the Messiah.[10]

---

[9] Marcus Borg, *Jesus and Buddha: The Parallel Sayings*, Berkeley, Seastone/Ulysses Press, 1997, pp. v-vi, viii.

[10] One reason for this is that in the two earliest "source" Gospels (the *Synoptic Sayings Source* and the earliest layer of *The Gospel of Thomas*) Jesus makes no references to himself.

They insist that such notions sprang from the faith of later Christians who gradually began to think of Jesus as a divinity.

Most scholars consider Jesus' "I am" statements in *The Gospel of John* to be the words of the Christian author, not the words of the historical Jesus. But Jesus the mystic might have said words very similar to these, and those words may have been misconstrued. Is it not possible that Jesus said something like "I and the Father are one," and meant it in the same way Krishna did?

The numerous "I am" statements from the Gnostic Gospels can only be understood properly by realizing that the speaker (or author) is merely channeling the voice of God. Certainly the Gnostic-Christian who put the following words into Jesus' mouth understood Jesus this way:

> I am the Light above everything; I am the All; all came forth from me and all has returned to me. Split the wood and I am there. Lift up the stone and you will find Me there.[11]

In the Bagavad Gita, Krishna teaches Arjuna, "Tat tvam Asi," "Thou art That." Atman (the Self, or soul) *is* Brahman (God). The being-ness of the individual is inextricably connected to "Being" itself. Since the essence of the individual, the Self or Atman, is divine, it is also immortal. While the physical body and one's ego-identity are subject to birth, decay, and extinction, nothing can harm the Spirit within. This Atman, this Self, is never born, thus it can never die. Jesus said much the same thing: "Fear not those who can kill the body but

cannot kill the soul" (*Matthew* 10:28; Luke 12:4).

But, the Semitic religions—Judaism, Christianity and Islam—do not believe that we are part of God. Indeed, such an idea is the ultimate heresy. Since Jesus was a Jew, any claim he

---

[11] *The Gospel of Thomas*, 77.

might have made that suggested oneness with God would have been considered blasphemous. Judaism did not accept such a premise two thousand years ago, and it does not accept it today.

In modern times, the case for the Jewish rejection of monism was made clear in *I and Thou*, a book written by the Jewish philosopher, Martin Buber, in 1958. Buber's point of view was exactly the opposite of Krishna's. Buber insisted that there were not one, but two realities in the Universe: God, and God's creation. By their very nature, Buber argued, these two realities could never be one and the same. No part of God's creation could *become* God. And while we—part of God's creation—could have a *relationship* with God, we could come no closer to Him. I *and* Thou, could never become I *am* Thou.

Monism and dualism represent two mutually exclusive, fundamentally incompatible, cosmologies. Certainly there have been mystics in Judaism, Christianity and Islam who have experienced a personal identity with the All. But in order to avoid charges of heresy, they walked a very fine line when attempting to communicate their mystical insights within the confines of their religion's dogma. They had no choice but to hide their monistic insights within the language of dualism.

Eastern Philosophy and Gnostic Christianity

If Jesus was not directly influenced by Eastern philosophy, there is the strong possibility that Gnostic Christianity was. Although the Gnostic Gospels are full of strange cosmologies

and life-denying philosophy, it is still possible to recognize the influence of the Eastern worldview.

In the Gnostic Gospels the historical Jesus is somewhat irrelevant, just as he is for Paul, the self-proclaimed apostle of Christ. Here, Jesus is always to be thought of as the Christ, the avatar of God who came to awaken humanity from its sleep, not the flesh and blood teacher from Galilee. All the dialogue that takes place between Jesus and the disciples in the Gnostic Gospels takes place after the crucifixion. This is not the historical Jesus speaking; this is the risen Christ. Here, Jesus is more of a spiritual presence than a physical one.

Except for specific sayings in *The Gospel of Thomas*, the Gnostic Gospels do not help us understand who the historical Jesus was. The Gnostic Christ is like the Hindu Krishna in the Bagavad Gita—a mythical avatar through whom the Godhead speaks. It is God who, time after time, in countless forms, through countless ages, reveals Himself in flesh, or in the of the appearance flesh—and walks among us.

> I am in everything. I uphold the heavens, I am the foundation which supports the planets, I am the Light that shines everywhere, that gives joy to souls. I am the life of the world: I am the sap in trees, and the sweet water that lies beneath the children of matter.
>
> – *Manichean Psalter*

> I am the origin of all things. In me the whole universe originates and dissolves…All this is strung in Me, as a row of jewels on a thread. I am the wetness of

water…the radiance in the moon and the sun…I am the sweet fragrance in earth, and the brilliance in fire am I: the life in all beings…

– *The Bagavad Gita*

The Gnostic Jesus teaches many of the same things that Krishna does: The world is an illusion. All created things are impermanent, so being attached to them is pointless. The purpose of life is to attain knowledge (gnosis), an experiential realization that the Self that lies within us all is truly divine substance. Atman is Brahman. The Self *is* God.

For orthodox Christianity, the human condition is due to original sin. For Gnostic-Christians, the human condition—including disease and death—is due to ignorance: ignorance of one's own divine nature. Thus, the Gnostic Christ did not appear on earth to save humanity from sin and death. Christ came to dispel ignorance and illusion, and to lead those who had awakened back home to God.

Like Krishna, Christ taught that humanity's ignorance and alienation from the All was the result of attraction to, and desire for, the impermanent pleasures of the material world—something the historical Jesus taught as well. The way out of this dilemma is in renouncing the world of impermanence, dedicating one's life to the job of attaining gnosis, and unifying and purifying the Self within.

The Gnostic Christ (and the historical Jesus), like the Buddha, like Krishna, like Lao Tzu, taught that all material things are impermanent—whether they be riches, or one's own body. Attachment to that which is impermanent causes suffering. Give up attachment and suffering ceases.

Like Lao Tzu, the Gnostic Jesus taught that the created order was manifested in pairs of opposites: yin and yang, light and darkness, good and evil, life and death, love and hate, male and female. This Jesus taught that in order to attain unity with God once more, it was necessary to unite the opposites—within and without, above and below. A single, spiritual, eye must take the place of eyes. The masculine and feminine aspects of the individual must be united into a single, androgynous, Being. According to the Gnostic interpretation of the Genesis creation story, Eve's creation from Adam's rib was a metaphor for the split within human consciousness. The Gnostic Christ taught that gnosis and inner harmony—reentry to the Garden of Eden—could only be achieved by reintegrating our masculine and feminine natures.

At least some—perhaps all—of the various schools of Gnostic Christianity believed in reincarnation. And there is no question that they all believed that the soul was immortal. But the most important parallel between Gnostic Christianity and Eastern religions is the emphasis upon attaining enlightenment in this lifetime. The great quest of Hinduism, Buddhism and Gnostic Christianity is to seek and find the means for liberating oneself from the bonds of the material, illusory, world.

Such liberation in all traditions is not through grace, but through individual effort, and only through individual effort. While Gnostic-Christians accepted the crucifixion of Jesus, they gave no theological meaning to that terrible event—except in proposing that Jesus left his body and did not really suffer on the cross.

As for the resurrection of Jesus, Gnostic-Christians considered it a spiritual, not physical, event. For the individual Christian, resurrection of the dead was not something that would take place at the end of time. Resurrection in Christ was something that took place here and now, a new state of consciousness which did not change when the physical body died.

For early "orthodox" Christianity, Gnostic Christianity was the ultimate heresy. And nothing would make an early Church father see red faster than suggesting that Jesus didn't suffer on the cross. For Eastern philosophy and for Gnostic Christianity, suffering is a limitation and something to overcome. But for Christian orthodoxy, suffering is the *point*. Mel Gibson—a Roman Catholic—made that very clear in his movie, *The Passion of the Christ*.

This raises other questions: Can we consider Gnostic Christianity a valid form of Christianity? Could it claim the right to speak for Jesus in the same way orthodoxy could? Did it have any relationship to "original" Christianity?

It is important to understand that neither form of Christianity had much to do with the historical Jesus, or the original Jesus movement that formed around him both before and immediately after his crucifixion. This movement, with its headquarters in Jerusalem, died out after 70 C.E. when the Romans destroyed Jerusalem and the first great Jewish Diaspora took place. After this date, only Christianity

existed. Early Christianity was not one movement, but many. There were virtually hundreds of early gospels, and each of them represented a different form of Christian faith. Over time, however, only two forms of Christianity survived and battled for supremacy.

The Church has always taught that Gnostic Christianity was a late heretical movement, but scholars now know better. There is evidence in Paul's letters to the Corinthians, Galatians and Philippians, that some of the Christians Paul refers to as "false apostles" preaching "false gospels" were actually Gnostic-Christian missionaries. If this is true, then Gnostic Christianity developed at the very same time as Paul's supposedly "orthodox" version did.

In addition, the *New Testament* book, *Acts of the Apostles*, contains references to the two original founders of Gnosticism: Simon Magus and Nicolas. In *Acts*, Nicolas was one of the first seven deacons elected to run the financial affairs of the first Jesus community in Jerusalem. Simon Magus was a former magician, Christian convert and mythological adversary of Simon Peter.

In addition to these references, there is also mention—in the form of a condemnation—of the Nicolaitanes (the supposedly heretical sect founded by Nicolas)—in the *New Testament Book of Revelations*. While the stories themselves probably have little historical value, they prove that both orthodox and Gnostic forms of Christianity originated at the same time.

One further piece of evidence is worthy of note: *The Gospel of Thomas* (the full text of which was discovered at Nag

Hammadi in 1945) is generally considered a Gnostic-Christian text. But it contains formerly unknown sayings which scholars are now certain come from the historical Jesus. It also contains *earlier versions* of sayings that have parallels in the canonical Gospels. This historical layer of *Thomas* is dated to 50 C.E., making it the earliest known Gospel, and contemporary with Paul's letters—which are dated between 50 C.E. and 65 C.E.

Besides the *Gospel of Thomas*, there are other Gnostic and apocryphal texts attributed to the disciple, Thomas, and scholars believe that they all originated within a community formed around Thomas. It is interesting to note that in Church tradition, Thomas was the disciple tasked with taking the Christian Gospel to India. This tradition seems to have some historical foundation since there are still traces of a Thomas tradition in India today. It is unlikely that Thomas himself ever traveled to India, but Thomas Christians did.

Because of such new discoveries many scholars are now making the argument that Gnostic Christianity can be considered just as original and just as valid as orthodoxy. In fact, had it not been for the fourth century Roman emperor, Constantine—who sided with the orthodox Church and persecuted Gnostic-Christians out of existence—this mystical form of Christianity might still be practiced today.

How would our society differ today had this been the case? Would society be different if our culture and religion encouraged intuitive awareness instead of intellectual analysis? Would our nation's foreign policies differ if they were based on a unified worldview instead of xenophobia and self-interest? And might our own lives be different had we been encouraged from birth to seek God consciousness instead of worshipping a distant patriarchal judge of the Universe?

Up until this point we've discussed the teachings of Jesus, Buddha, Krishna and Lao Tzu only in terms of theology and philosophy—both of which are intellectual exercises which, in themselves, are empty of reality. Now let's look at them from a mystic's vantage point—as personal aspects of our own experience.

Let Me Take You Higher

> …it is easier to sail many thousand miles through cold and storm and cannibals, in a government ship, with five hundred men and boys to assist one, than it is to explore the private sea, the Atlantic and Pacific Ocean of one's being alone.
>
> – Henry David Thoreau, *Walden*

While Christianity has produced its own mystics over the centuries, orthodox theologians have rarely placed any value on the contemplative life—and certainly not upon its perceptions of reality. They have somehow been able to "work around" all those teachings of Jesus that support a mystical worldview.

It doesn't seem to occur to the average theologian that his or her premises are based entirely upon intellectual concepts which are themselves a product of ordinary waking consciousness—as if this were the only valid form of consciousness. From that perspective, certainly, everything in the Universe does appear to be separate and apart.

This self-imposed limitation leaves theologians with no other choice but to consider mystical insights, whether naturally or chemically induced, to be hallucinogenic. This is ironic given that mystics insist just the opposite: it is "normal" consciousness that produces an illusory world. What we know from modern science (or at least what science tells us) is that all forms of consciousness are the result of chemical interactions within the human brain. If "higher" levels of conscious—or altered states—are hallucinations, then, so are our everyday thoughts!

Better living through chemistry is the order of the day. We take one pill to pump us up, another to calm us down. Overly anxious? Don't worry, we've got a pill for that. Depressed? Just take some of these and you'll feel happy again in about two weeks. Have a fear of flying? Ask the flight attendant for a couple shots of Jack Daniels and you'll love the experience.

Today, we think nothing of altering our brain chemistry in order to better cope with life. Yet our society has a taboo against doing the same thing for religious purposes. This attitude overlooks the fact that when it comes to consciousness—chemicals, the human brain, and religious experience have always gone hand in hand.

Many New Testament scholars, for instance, believe that the apostle Paul's out-of-body experiences were brought on by epileptic seizures—which, in turn, were brought about by chemical shifts within the brain. William James pointed out more than a century ago that even alcohol can induce mystical raptures.

Since human perception is dependent upon chemical reactions within the brain, we can never know—objectively—just what "real" reality is. We can never know, and certainly never prove, that our reality is the same as the next person's. We must, if we are honest, rephrase Descartes famous dictum from "cogito ergo sum!" to "cogito ergo sum, cogito!" I think, therefore I am—I think.

For now though, critics of altered states of consciousness argue that episodes of mystical awareness are either unnaturally induced—and, therefore, invalid—or are purely accidental—which also makes them invalid. But I think it is safe to say that those who make this judgment have never taken "a trip around the head" as Timothy Leary used to put it. It's not likely that very many scientists have ever had a mystical experience, with or without drugs. As human beings, we all seem to operate on the principle that only our own experiences of reality are legitimate, while the other guy's are delusional.

Those of us who were participants in the psychedelic era of the 1960s no longer look at reality that way. Because we took the magical mystery tour, most of our lives were altered dramatically as a result. No, we didn't go insane or destroy all of our brain cells. Rather—and this is just a personal opinion—we simply became more perceptive human beings.

This might not have been the case at all were it not for the fact that the psychedelic era coincided with an invasion of spiritual gurus from the East. Those who claimed that higher consciousness could be achieved *naturally* came to America at the precise moment the Counter Culture discovered marijuana, LSD, peyote, psilocybin and mescaline. The combination of these two forces ultimately altered the face of Western religion.

During the 1950s, Western students and teachers of Eastern philosophy, such as Alan Watts, paved the way for psychologists like Richard Alpert to become Ram Dass during the '60s. Ram Dass was able to communicate with an entire generation of spiritual seekers and make spiritual sense out of the drug-induced mystical experiences they were having, precisely because he, too, had experienced the same altered states of consciousness.

Dr. Alpert's scientific experiments with LSD at Harvard got him fired along with Dr. Timothy Leary and Dr. Ralph Metzner. Alpert then went to India where he met his guru, Neum Karoi Baba, who gave him the spiritual name of Baba Ram Dass.

My favorite story in Ram Dass' classic first book, *Be Here Now*, was when Neum Karoli Baba asked the then Dr. Richard Alpert for some of his "medicine." Since the request was made through an interpreter, Alpert didn't understand what the guru wanted at first. Finally it became clear that the guru was asking for some LSD, which Alpert had with him. Alpert considered this an odd request, even a potentially harmful one. But the guru kept holding out his hand, so Ram Dass finally gave him a tab of the magical drug.

One serving was more than enough "acid" for a good, and usually safe, twelve hour "trip." But instead of swallowing the LSD, the guru held out his hand for more. Now Alpert really started to become apprehensive. What would happen if this guru flipped out? He would be to blame. Alpert tried to explain the situation through the interpreter, but still the guru was insistent, so Alpert gave him another dose.

Neum Karoli, however, indicated that he wanted even more. In the end, Richard Alpert gave the guru enough LSD to send him off into another universe with no return ticket. The guru smiled and popped the handful of mind-bending acid into his mouth and swallowed.

Feeling extremely uncomfortable, Richard Alpert could only wait to see what would happen when the LSD (which takes about an hour to start working) took effect. An hour passed, with no change. The guru just sat there in a lotus posture and smiled ("twinkled," as Ram Dass later put it.) Two hours passed, three. Still, Alpert saw no change! Neum Karoli Baba never moved from his full lotus posture, and simply continued to "twinkle."

Ram Dass' point in telling this story was simply to illustrate that Neum Karoli Baba's consciousness was so far beyond normal, that even a handful of mind-altering chemicals had no effect on it. The answer to expanded consciousness, Dr. Alpert suddenly understood, was *not* to be found in drugs. Richard Alpert, former professor, former Jewish psychologist, became the disciple of a guru dressed in rags—and it changed his life forever.

Many, perhaps most, of us who experimented with psychedelic drugs during that era also turned to Eastern religions for answers. Why?—because those religions are all *about* altered states of consciousness. Judaism, Christianity and Islam teach God, but Eastern religions teach God *consciousness*. The Counter Culture needed to understand the meaning of their drug-induced experiences. Synagogues, churches and mosques offered no answers.

> According to the drug cultists, men today are thirsting for the direct, personal experience of God—regardless of his actual nature. In other words, it matters not whether God lies within or without; in either case, men need and want a sense of direct communion with the ultimate source of their faith. The divine-human encounter is not found in church, where little or nothing is done to promote it. But it is found in LSD, the cultists believe. Thus LSD challenges the church to do as well and offer as much.[12]

It has been forty years since those words were written, and it is important to note that there is no longer a "LSD cult," if there ever was one. It did not take many young people very long to figure out that drugs were a dead end. What goes up must come down. If drugs couldn't maintain one's high, perhaps meditation and yoga could.

One did not need to have an experience of God to appreciate the value of altered states of consciousness. The first time I took LSD, I merely watched a sunset at the beach in an indescribable state of bliss. A sunset over the ocean is always a beautiful sight. This was something far better.

Back at home, the usual mess left by my roommates did not bother me at all. In fact, everything looked perfect just the way it was—not an insignificant revelation for an anal-retentive personality. LSD and marijuana taught me one important lesson: reality can be perceived on many different levels. Everyday consciousness is simply the default consciousness evolution hard-wired into our brains—no doubt because it ensures our physical survival. Otherwise, it is no better or worse than any other type of consciousness.

I first recognized altered states of consciousness some years earlier—and without the aid of drugs. If the experience I had then cannot be classified as mystical, it certainly qualified for what the psychologist, Abraham Maslow, called a "peak experience."

I had taken a year off after my second year of college to earn enough money to continue, but also because my previous career goal had gone down the tubes. Suddenly, I hadn't the faintest idea what I should do with my life. Worse still, I was pressuring myself unmercifully to figure it out, and quickly. But after half of this year had gone by, I still didn't have a clue.

On this particular day, I was helping my parents by pulling weeds in their rose garden. My mind was dwelling on my predicament, and I was feeling confused and rather despondent. Suddenly a voice came into my mind, saying

---

[12] William Braden, *The Private Sea, LSD and the Search for God*, Chicago, Bantom Books, 1968, p. 4.

23

something like, "You will serve Me for the rest of your life. You will be a minister to My people."

I experienced no burning bush. I wasn't blinded by the light. And I was fully aware that God's "voice" was coming from some deep place within myself. Even so, it overpowered me. I had never before considered studying for the ministry. The thought had never entered my mind until this very moment. I didn't think I was crazy enough to come up with an idea like this on my own, so whether it was God or my subconscious advising me, I was still incredulous.

The Voice persisted, but I told it in no uncertain terms, and in a dozen different ways, that it had the wrong guy. I wasn't smart enough. I wasn't holy enough. I wasn't devoted enough, and on and on and on. But God, my subconscious, whatever it was, countered my every argument and excuse. I felt like Jacob wrestling with an angel.

Finally, I could resist no longer and simply gave up. I surrendered to what I considered to be God's will. This complete letting go of my own will overwhelmed me with relief. I don't know how long I knelt there in the dirt, sobbing, but it was quite some time.

Finally, the tears ceased flowing, I stood up, and the world was transformed before my eyes! Everything looked glorious and new, and I felt like I had entered the Kingdom of God. Of course I knew the world was no different than before, but my perception of it had changed completely.

I was low man on the totem pole where I had been working during this year, and I had to take flak not only from the boss, but from clerks and from customers as well—a perfect situation for someone with a generally grumpy mood and a critical state of mind. But now all of those negative traits suddenly disappeared.

For the next seven days, there was nothing but love in my heart and on my lips. Absolutely nothing bothered me. I was unable to become angry or upset or depressed—not even for a moment. As a consequence, every word that came out of my mouth, every action I took, came from a place of pure love. I had been transformed! I had achieved sainthood in the blink of an eye!

When I woke up the morning of the eighth day, however, Saint Richard was gone. And for the past four decades I have grieved over the loss of him. But even though I had fallen back to Earth, I now *knew* what Jesus meant when he talked about being born anew. I knew what he meant when he spoke of the Kingdom of God. The Kingdom was not a metaphor, it was a *reality*. Grace had allowed me to glimpse Paradise through a window. It was now up to me to find the door so that I might enter.

Many of us in modern times have taken similar journeys. Our paths have brought us together—to this very moment, when we hold in our hands some of the greatest spiritual wisdom the world has ever known. These words are more than inspiration. They are signposts along the road that will lead us back home.

"What you are looking

for is what is looking."

– St. Francis of Assisi

*"All you who seek
the Way please,
do not waste this
moment now."*

– *Zen teaching*

THE GREAT WAY

"The mountain is the mountain
And the Way is the same as of old.
Verily what is changed
Is my own heart."

— *Anonymous*

The Way spoken of by the world's great teachers is not one single path, yet all paths lead to the same destination. Traveled by the pilgrim, the Way is the path to Life. It is the quest for our own personal holy grail. The Way stretches out before us, endless. It leads beyond the horizon, yet it begins with a single step.

Once the Way is chosen, there is no turning back. We may stop and rest awhile. We may tarry here and there for as long as necessary. We may even fall asleep by the side of the road. But we will eventually awaken no matter how long we sleep. Then, recognizing that the day's shadows are falling long across the path, we stir ourselves, cinch up our belts, and continue on.

If we do not know where the Way begins, there are those who can show us. If we become lost, there are those who can give us directions. If we need company, there are those who will be our traveling companions. But they can walk with us just so far. Eventually they must part, bidding us good journey, knowing that the path we travel is a path we must take alone.

✦ ✦ ✦

The *New Testament* book, *Acts of the Apostles*, tells us that sometime after the death of Jesus, his friends and disciples formed a community in Jerusalem. The name of this community, Acts tells us, was called "the Way." This gathering of the Way was not a Christian community, however, because Christianity had yet to be invented. Rather, the Way was the religion *of* Jesus, not the later religion *about* him.

Acts of the Apostles tells us that Saul of Tarsus, later to become Paul, the apostle of Christ, initially persecuted the Way: "...if he found any belonging to the Way, men or women, he might bring them bound to Jerusalem." (Acts 9:2). Later, the author of *Acts* has Paul say, "I persecuted the Way to death" (Acts 22:4).

Acts leads us to believe that Paul—once he renounced his old ways and began preaching his unique gospel of the Christ—became the friend and co-worker of the leaders of the Way in Jerusalem: James, the brother of Jesus, Simon Peter and John. But the author of *Acts*—written around the end of the first century—was trying to rehabilitate Paul's reputation as an adversary of these men.

In the letter to his church in Galacia, Paul wrote that, three years after his "conversion," he went to Jerusalem, hoping to work hand in hand with James, Peter and John.

But in the end, the differences between Paul and the leaders of the Way turned out to be irreconcilable. Paul finally opposed these men openly, and after he verbally attacked Peter in Antioch, the followers of the Way went one direction, and Paul's Christianity went another (Galatians 1:11—2:14).

Nevertheless, *Acts* insists that Paul himself taught "the Way"

(Acts 19:9; 19:23). He even insists that Paul was a Nazarene like Jesus (Acts 24:5), then states that the sect of the Nazarenes and the sect of "the Way" were one and the same (Acts 24:14).

Finally, the author of *Acts* mentions "the Way" one last time when he tells the story of Paul's trial for heresy. Antonius Felix, procurator of Judea, under whom Paul was being tried on this occasion, was himself said to have "accurate knowledge of the Way" (Acts 24:21), and apparently Paul didn't measure up.

While "the Way," as a designation for Jesus' particular wisdom tradition, appears in *Acts of the Apostles* seven times, these references alone are not sufficient evidence that Jesus' disciples were actually known by this name—since the name appears nowhere else in the *New Testament*. Yet Jesus *did use* the term when describing the difficulty of the spiritual path:

> Enter by the narrow gate; for the gate is wide and the way is easy, that leads to destruction, and those who enter by it are many. For the gate is narrow and the way is hard, that leads to Life. And those who find it are few.
>
> – *Matthew* 7:13; *Luke* 13:24

Hsin Hsin Ming, the Third Chinese Patriarch of Zen, blended Taoism with Buddhism, and his commentary on the Great Way offers a different perspective:

> The Way is not difficult for those who have no preferences. When love and hate are both absent,

everything becomes clear and undisguised. Make the following distinction, however, and heaven and earth are set infinitely apart.

If you wish to see the truth, then hold no opinions for or against anything. To set up what you like against what you dislike is the disease of the mind.

This is a true statement, but there's a catch. Who among us has no preferences? Who does not discriminate? Who does not hold opinions? It takes a lifetime of spiritual work to develop the dispassion that Hsin Ming speaks of, and only a small minority of people in every age will do so. So the Zen Patriarch's statement is full of irony. He is telling us how life could be—how easy the spiritual path would be—if we no longer made distinctions between things. Jesus and Hsin Ming are saying the same thing in different ways.

For Lao Tzu and Taoism, the Way includes the meaning of "spiritual path," but infers a great deal more. Tao, the Way, is the *flow* of life. It is the "way of things." It is the force that moves in all things, permeates all things, governs all things. The Way cannot be manipulated, nor can it be resisted. It cannot even be known.

Tao will do what Tao does. As little people in the vast scheme of things, we succeed in life only when we let Tao flow through us, and around us, freely. Conversely, we make a good deal of trouble for ourselves every time we attempt to resist the ways of Tao. Can we make the wind stop blowing?

Lao Tzu tells us that we can only be happy, and the things

we do can only be successful, if we *yield* to Tao—surrender to the way things are. Rather than a great tree resisting the wind, and sometimes breaking, we should become like bamboo, yielding and supple. Then the wind will flow through unhindered, and bamboo will not break. Happiness in life is the result of accepting everything just the way it is. Serenity is achieved when one no longer wishes for "something else."

The principle of the Great Way applies to the individual, but it also applies to nations. Lao Tzu tells us that any nation that resists change will eventually doom itself. Any ruler who does not govern the people according to the principles of the Way will ruin both the nation and himself. Today we say, "Go with the flow." If we want inner peace and outer harmony in society, we have to learn not to push the river.

To live in the Way, *we* must get out of the way. We cannot grasp the Way, so we must accept it with humility. And the more we simplify our lives—the more we bring it in alignment with Tao—the richer our lives will be.

The Buddha agreed: "If you seek to embrace the Way through the path of learning, the Way will not be understood. If you observe the Way with simplicity of heart, great indeed is the Way." Krishna says this also: "Both lust and aversion to the things of nature arise from man's lower nature. Do not come under their powers. These are enemies of the Way."

Lao Tzu often refers to Tao as the "Way of heaven." Jesus called Tao, the Kingdom of heaven, or the Kingdom of God. Later orthodox Christians misunderstood Jesus' teaching about the Kingdom and believed that it was some sort of perfected world which would be ushered in at the end of time. Jesus, however, taught that the Kingdom was already here—here, there, everywhere! To recognize the Way, the Kingdom, one needs to develop eyes that see and ears that hear. And if we do, we will discover that the Kingdom, the Way of heaven is not only everywhere around us, it is within us as well.

JESUS	KRISHNA
The Kingdom is spread out over the whole world, and people do not see it. *- The Gospel of Thomas*	What use is a reservoir where there is a flood everywhere? *- The Upanishads*
Ask, and it will be given you. Seek, and you will find. Knock, and the door will be opened. *- The Gospel of Matthew*	Hear now of that Way that the wise men of the Vedas called eternal. *- The Upanishads*
Judas asked, "How does one begin to walk the Way?" Jesus answered, "By developing love and compassion." *- The Dialogue of the Savior*	The one who has good will for all, who is friendly and has compassion…and forgiveness…comes to Me. *- Bagavad Gita*
The Kingdom is not coming with signs to be observed. The Kingdom of God is within you. *- The Gospel of Luke*	Those who seek oneness ceaselessly find the Lord dwelling in their own hearts. *- The Bagavad Gita*
This Way you have found, even the angels do not know it. It comes from the unity of the Father and the Son, for they are One. Travel this path you have found. *- The Dialogue of the Savior*	I have revealed to you the most secret doctrine… He who has seen it has seen Light, and his work in this life is finished. *- The Bagavad Gita*

BUDDHA	LAO TZU
The Way is complete in itself. Like the vastness of space, it lacks nothing, and has nothing in excess. *- The Third Chinese Patriarch of Zen*	The Great Way is abundant on all sides. Everything comes from it, and no sentient being is denied its blessings. Calling none its own, it feeds and clothes everyone. *- The Tao Te Ching*
Listen avidly to and cherish the Way which is called mighty. *- The Sutra of Forty-Two Sections*	In ancient times, how was Tao honored by men of wisdom? Did they not declare that it might be found by seekers? *- The Tao Te Ching*
Only those with a pure heart, and with a single purpose, will be able to understand the most supreme Way. *- The Kevaddha Sutta*	The man of virtue discovers the Way. Those with faults are forgiven. This is why Tao is such a treasure. *- The Tao Te Ching*
To begin the journey in the Way...first, set yourself straight. You are your only master. *- The Dhammapada*	The Way is empty, yet contains all. Words cannot describe it. Better that one should look for it within. *- The Tao Te Ching*
The Way cannot be found in words. Nothing on earth can define it. If one loses sight of it, even for an instant, it may be lost forever. *- The Buddha*	The secret waits for those who have no desire. *- The Tao Te Ching*

JESUS	KRISHNA
When I came among humanity I opened the door to the Way and revealed the path that must be traveled. Those who follow are the chosen ones who have sought unity within themselves. They understood the truth because they have known the Father. *- The Dialogue of the Savior*	The light which resides in the sun and shines on all...is My light. Entering the earth with My energy, I support all beings, and I nourish all the herbs, becoming the watery moon. *- The Bagavad Gita*
I am the way, the truth, and the life. *- The Gospel of John*	Many are the paths of men, though all those paths end in Me for those who love Me. *- The Bagavad Gita*
Open the door of the Way within yourself so that you may guide those who wish to follow you through it. Reward all those who are ready to receive their reward. *- The Second Apocalypse of James*	God allowed man to look outward, but seeing the outer, the inner was ignored. Some wise man seeking eternal life turned his sight within, and beheld his own Spirit. *- The Katha Upanishad*
You have me for a couch. Rest yourself upon Me. *- The Hymn of Jesus from The Acts of John*	Whoever comes to Me for shelter, they will all reach the Way supreme. *- Bagavad Gita*
The Kingdom is within you, and one who knows oneself will find it. *- Papyrus Oxyrhynchus*	When the five senses and the mind are stilled, when the reasoning intellect rests in silence, then begins the highest path. *- The Katha Upanishad*

BUDDHA	LAO TZU
Those who are pure in heart and single in purpose are able to understand the most supreme Way. It is like polishing a mirror, which becomes bright when the dust is removed. *- The Dhammapada*	I ask for understanding as I travel the great Way, so that I might not lose sight of the road. The great Way is simple and manifest, but people prefer to take other paths. *- The Tao Te Ching*
Cross the river, leave the raft behind and proceed. This is the way I have taught you. *- Majjhima Nikaya*	The mighty way is easy underfoot, but people still prefer the little paths. *- The Tao Te Ching*
Looking within, finding stillness—free from fear, free from attachment—know the sweet joy of the Way. *- The Dhammapada*	The sage knows himself, but makes no show of himself. He loves himself, but does not exalt himself. He prefers what is within to what is without. *- The Tao Te Ching*
I go to the Buddha for refuge. *- The Khuddakapatha*	Do not try to hold onto the Way. Just hope the Way will hold on to you. *- Chuang Tzu*
It is good to practice the Way and follow truth. It is even better to have one's heart in harmony with the Way. *- The Kevaddha Sutta*	

JESUS	KRISHNA
I am a beacon to those who see Me. I am a mirror to those who look at Me. I am a door to those who knock on Me. I am a Way to you the traveler. *- The Hymn of Jesus from The Acts of John*	I am the Way, and the Master who watches in silence— your friend, your shelter, your dwelling of peace. I am the beginning and the end of all things—the seed of eternity, and the treasure supreme. *- The Bagavad Gita*
Enter by the narrow gate; for the gate is wide and the way is easy, that leads to destruction, and those who enter by it are many. For the gate is narrow and the Way is hard, that leads to life. And those who find it are few. *- The Gospels of Matthew; Luke*	There are two paths that are forever: the path of darkness and the path of light. The one leads to the land of no returning. The other leads to sorrow. *- The Bagavad Gita*
Many are called but few are chosen. *- The Gospel of Matthew*	The Way of the transcendent is hard for mortals to attain. *- The Bagavad Gita*
Make haste to follow the Way, which is direct, straight and narrow. *- The Epistula Apostolorum*	Let the wise…seek that Way wherefrom those who go, never return. *- The Bagavad Gita*
The son of Man is within you. Follow Him. *- The Gospel of Mary*	Seen in a vision of wonder, this is the Way of righteousness. Follow it, for it leads to the highest goal. *- The Bagavad Gita*

BUDDHA	LAO TZU
The most supreme among humanity are those who have eyes to see. This is the Way, and there is no other that leads to purifying the intellect. Take that path! *- The Dhammapada*	When the wise man hears of the Way, he works hard to apply it. When the mediocre person hears of it, he keeps it then loses it. But when the ignorant hear of it, they laugh. If they did not laugh, it would not be the Way. *- The Tao Te Ching*
The followers of the Way are like dry straw, and must be protected against the fires of desire. One must put distance between oneself and the object of his desire. *- The Sutra of Forty-Two Sections*	If your actions are in accord with the Way, you will be of the Way. ...Nurture the Way yourself, and virtue will follow. *- The Tao Te Ching*
It is hard for the strong and rich to observe the Way. *- The Kavaddha Sutta*	The Way receives with gladness those who walk in its way... Abandonment will greet those who abandon it. *- Tao Te Ching*
To live in the great Way is neither easy nor difficult, but those with limited views are fearful and irresolute. *- Third Chinese Patriarch of Zen*	If you seek to embrace the Way through the path of learning, the Way will not be understood. If you observe the Way with simplicity of heart, great indeed is the Way. *- The Tao Te Ching*
To follow the Way is goodness. To have the will in conformity with the Way is greatness. *- The Sutra of Forty-Two Sections*	

JESUS	KRISHNA
Save for yourself only those things in life that will follow you. Seek and find this, and let all of your speech come from this place of harmony within you. You must know that the living God is within you and you are in him. *- The Dialog of the Savior*	Attachment and aversion of the senses for their respective objects is natural. Do not come under their powers. These are enemies of the Way. *- The Bagavad Gita*
Do not seek your salvation because others urge you. Let the motivation to find it come from within you. *- The Apocryphon of James*	Who everywhere is free from all ties, who neither rejoices nor sorrows if fortune is good or ill, he has serene wisdom. *- The Bagavad Gita*
You must unify that which is outside of you with that which is within; that which is above you with that which is below. You must make the male and female one and the same. Then you will enter the Kingdom. *- The Second Apocalypse of James*	The yogi who knows these paths no longer lives in delusion. Be one, therefore, with yoga (union.) *- The Bagavad Gita*
A sower went out to sow. As he sowed, some seed fell along the path, and birds devoured it. Other seed fell on rocky ground where there was no soil...Still other seed fell among thorns, which choked it. Yet other seed fell onto good soil and brought forth grain, growing up and increasing...one hundred-fold. *- The Gospels of Matthew, Mark, Luke and Thoma*	

BUDDHA	LAO TZU
Those who seek to make a name for themselves, but neglect to study the Way, are waging battles against empty forms. *- The Sutra in Forty-Two Sections*	If you consider riches and honor to be important, you will only bring calamity upon yourselves. The Way of heaven is this: when you have done your work, retire! *- The Tao Te Ching*
The Way is perfect...Be serene in the oneness of things. *- The Third Chinese Patriarch of Zen*	The Way is a void. It is used but never filled up... It is a deep pool that never runs dry. *- The Tao Te Ching*
No one under heaven is able to become a follower of the Way if he accepts dualism. *- The Sutra of Forty-Two Sections*	The Way can be compared to the rushing torrents that flow from rivers into the sea. *- The Tao Te Ching*
Those who follow the Way are like warriors who fight single-handed against many foes. They leave the fort in full armor, but some of them are faint of heart and eventually retreat. Others are killed, while still others return home victorious. *- The Buddha*	

JESUS	KRISHNA

The kingdom of God does not come in such a way as to be seen. No one will say: "Here it is!" or "There it is!" Because the kingdom is within you.

- The Gospel of Luke

BUDDHA	LAO TZU

The Way is not in the sky. The Way is in the heart.
- *The Buddha*

One can know the world without leaving home.
The Way can be seen without a window.
- *The Tao Te Ching*

"Where is God? Your body is His moving temple. The Sanctum Sanctorum is the chamber of your own heart."

– Swami Sivananda

GOD, TAO AND UNIVERSAL MIND

"Vedanta says there is nothing that is not God…the living God is within you…the only God to worship is the human soul in the human body."

– *Swami Vivekananda*

Buddhism, many have said, is not so much a religion as it is a psychology. It is concerned with the workings of the human mind. Its business is helping people to "wake up," to provide the tools that allow one to expand their perception of reality. Buddhism may have all the trappings of a religion—robes, altars, incense, ritual—but even though it sometimes speaks of "Universal Mind," Buddhism does not posit the existence of God. Consequently, Buddhism has no theology—no "words about God." Does God exist? The Buddhist is likely to answer, "It really doesn't matter one way or another since the human predicament remains the same in either case. Our job is to dispel illusion and alleviate suffering."

Hindus would agree with Buddhists on this point—and it's useful to remember that Buddhism began as a Hindu sect—but when Hindus describe the process of enlightenment or "waking up," they are more likely to describe their experience of "Samadhi," or bliss consciousness, as being in the presence of God. Christians of all stripes—even mystics—also consider "God consciousness" as the goal of their inner quest.

Taoism represents yet another point of view. Tao is the force which permeates heaven and earth. Its ways can be known,

but not Tao itself. An ancient Taoist would probably tell us that further speculation about the "divine" nature of Tao would prove to be a waste of time.

Tao is an impersonal force in the Universe, just like Universal Mind. But, then, so is "God" in most, if not all, mystical traditions, including Hinduism and Gnostic-Christianity. Whatever word a mystic uses to describe Ultimate Reality, he or she is rarely speaking of a transcendent Being who created the Universe and micro-manages it.

Hinduism and Gnostic-Christianity (and perhaps mystical Christianity in general) use the word "God" to describe a Reality that, when examined closely, is far closer to the Universal Mind of Buddhism and the Tao of Taoism than it is to the personal God of Judaeo-Christianity and Islam.

Hindus, however, have no trouble at all personalizing the impersonal God. Their religion abounds with gods and goddesses. But this pantheon of deities—at least among the mystics of India—represents God's attributes, not individual deities. Those who developed Hinduism's pantheon of gods and goddesses many thousands of years ago were probably true polytheists. Over time, however, Hinduism evolved until it reached its greatest expression in the monastic philosophy of Vedanta, as expressed in its greatest scriptures, *The Upanishads* and *The Bagavad Gita*.

Being all things to all people, Hinduism never found the need to renounce its gods and goddesses. Even today many Hindus continue to worship their deities as they have for thousands of years. Even mystics do not find a dichotomy here, since Hinduism has always been tolerant of all expressions of religious faith. God can be one and many simultaneously.

Buddhism developed in the opposite direction. It began as a movement without deities of any kind, and only later took on all the trappings of religion. Originally, Buddhism was quite simple and straight forward, but the Mahayana—the "Great Vehicle"—school of Buddhism eventually evolved to accommodate, not just monks who were committed to renouncing the world, but also common people who carried on the usual affairs of daily life. With this change came a cosmos of deities over time. Had Buddhism not evolved in this manner, it may well have remained just one more Hindu sect or, perhaps, perished altogether.

Today, many Buddhists worship the historical Buddha much as Christians worship Christ: as a world savior (but not as God.) In addition, they give devotion to many other quasi-divine figures as well. Buddhism adopted and adapted as it moved out from India into the wider Asian world. In China, it absorbed philosophical Taoism, and reinvented itself as Zen Buddhism. When Buddhism came to Tibet in the seventh century C.E., it absorbed the indigenous religion of Bon, including its pantheon of deities and demons—which exist, but only in the world of appearance.

Gnosticism was such a diverse and complex religion that it is almost impossible to generalize about its theology. Gnostic-Christianity, as a religion in itself, adopted many Gnostic ideas, and rejected others, while giving it a unique Christian identity. In this, it was similar to Hinduism and Buddhism in adopting a cosmos full of demons and demi-gods. What set it apart from those religions, however, was the insistence that the various "powers" in the Universe conspired to keep humanity ignorant of its true divine origins.

Early "orthodox" Christians were abhorred by the Gnostic expression of Christian faith, especially its cosmos of evil forces which included the Hebrew creator-God, Yahweh. Yahweh, a demi-god unworthy of worship, played the part of a dungeon master by enslaving the divine soul in a prison of flesh.

Still, one has to wonder to what degree Gnostic-Christians literalized such powers, and to what degree they understood them as metaphors. Orthodox Christianity has always criticized Gnosticism in all of its forms as extreme "dualism," because it spoke of the true God as an "alien" force that exists far beyond the world of matter, and the human soul as a reality apart from the physical body.

Yet the concept of the soul in Gnosticism is little different from the concept of the immortal soul in Greek philosophy. Furthermore, for Gnostics, the world of matter didn't really exist apart from the All, the Godhead. Its separateness was merely "apparent." Ultimately, all things resolved themselves back into the All, and the Gnostic goal of joining the Self with the Godhead was, practically speaking, little different from the Hindu concept of Atman / Brahman. Ultimately, Hinduism, Buddhism, Taoism and Gnostic Christianity all teach that there is only one single Reality in the Universe, and nothing exists apart from It. In the end, the name we give this Reality—God, Brahman, Universal Mind, Tao or the All—is unimportant.

JESUS	KRISHNA
In the beginning was the Word, and the Word was with God, and the Word was God. He was in the beginning with God; all things through Him came into being, and without Him, nothing at all came into being. In Him was Life, and the Life became the light of men. And the Light appears in the darkness, and the darkness has not apprehended it. *- The Gospel of John*	Once, all was darkness. The All remained unseen within it, lacking distinct qualities, unknown and unknowable—as if in deep sleep. Then the Lord—who alone exists—became manifest along with His power. The self-existent Lord was everywhere, manifesting Himself from Himself. *- The Ordinances of Manu*
Before that which is visible came into being, all existed in Him, He embraces all, nothing embraces Him. *- The Sophia of Jesus Christ*	Before He manifested himself, He existed within Himself. Out of Himself, He manifested Himself. Thus, He is known as the Self-Existent One. *- Taittirya Upanishad*
I Am the one who is with you always. I am the Father, the Mother, the Son. I cannot be defiled or corrupted. I have come to teach you those things that are, and those things that will be, so that through this revelation you will perceive the perfection of humanity. *- The Apocryphon of John*	I Am the Soul that exists in everything. I am the beginning middle and end of all lives… I am mind dwelling in all living creatures. I am Light, consciousness, the eternal word. I am the One who never changes. I am lord over the future, and I am death. I am manifest in all things, and nothing moves without Me. *- The Bagavad Gita*

BUDDHA	LAO TZU

Universal Mind exists like a vast and boundless ocean. Waves disturb its surface, but beneath, all is calm and eternally unmoved. Having no personality, all things exist in it. But due to the disturbance upon its surface, it became an actor playing many parts.
- *The Lankavatara Sutra*

In the beginning there was the void, the One without name or form. In this One is the Being in whom all things exist. This is the Living One.
- *Chung Tzu*

I am not to be perceived by means of any visible form, Nor sought after by means of any audible sound; Whoever walks in the way of iniquity cannot perceive the blessedness of the Lord Buddha.
- *The Diamond Sutra*

The Great Tao pervades all things. It caused all things to come into existence.
- *The Tao Te Ching*

Mark well how varied are the aspects of the Immovable One, and know that the First Realty is unmoveable. Only when this insight is attained will the true workings of such-ness be understood.
- *A Manual on Zen Buddhism*

Something wonderful existed before heaven and earth were manifest. It is silent. It is sacred. It alone never changes. It acts, yet no actions accrue to it. It embraces all things with love, but asks nothing for itself. What name do I give this nameless One? I shall call it Tao, and glory in its power.
- *The Tao Te Ching*

JESUS	KRISHNA
The Word was made flesh, and dwelt among us. *- The Gospel of John*	All that is manifest is filled with God. All that is unmanifest is filled with God. From God all things flow. All things come from him, yet He alone does not change. *- Isha Upanishad*
The One that is undivided is ruled by none, and nothing exists above it. This One gave rise to all things, and through which all things came into being. The creator of all, uncorrupted, a pure Light into which no eyes can look. Unseen, He does not exist in things, but all things exist in Him. He is eternal, lacking nothing, complete and perfect. *- The Apocryphon of John*	The visible universe comes forth from Me who am invisible Being. All beings have their rest in Me, but I rest not in them. I am the Source of all beings. I support them all, yet I do not rest in them. At the end of the night of time all things return to Me. And with the dawn I bring them into the Light. *- The Bagavad Gita*
He that cannot be penetrated or divided, is He who exists as God, the Father of everything, the invisible One, above everything, uncorrupted. He is the pure light into which no eye can look. He is invisible Sprit. All things exist in Him, the Eternal—without limit, who cannot be sought or measured, who is invisible and ineffable. He is pure Mind. *- The Apocryphon of John*	In the heart of all things in the Universe, dwells the Lord. God alone is reality, so renounce appearances and delight in Him. *- Isha Upanishad*
Where there are three gods, they are gods. When there are two or one, I am with him. *- The Gospel of Thomas*	That one Thing, breathless, breathed by its own nature—apart from it nothing whatsoever exists. From this arose the primal seed and germ of spirit. *- The Rig Veda*

BUDDHA	LAO TZU
In Noble Wisdom, all things are in Nirvana from the beginning. *- The Lankavatara Sutra*	From ancient times to the present, taking on names without end, the Beginning was seen. How can I know the beginning of the All? How may I know its nature? Through Tao itself. *- The Tao Te Ching*
All living creatures born of every class, whether from eggs or from wombs, or from water, with form or without form, whether free or not free from thought, or beyond the worlds of thought—such things come from Me so that Nirvana might be attained. *- The Diamond Sutra*	All things exist in pairs and are dependent one on the other. This cannot exist without that. But what causes this? What power stands behind it all? I can see its works, yet I cannot see its form. *- Chuang Tzu*
Noble Wisdom is a state of perfection without images. It is the Womb of Such-ness." The essence of Divine Mind abides, undisturbed, eternally. *- The Lankavatara Sutra*	Tao can be talked about, but not the eternal Tao. Names can be given but not the eternal Name. The origin of heaven and earth is nameless—the mother of all things. As hidden we should look within. As revealed we should look without. These are mysteries. The mystery of mysteries is the Door of all essence. *- The Tao Te Ching*
	The Tao gave birth to the first principle. The first principle gave birth to duality which gave birth to the three. The three gave rise to all things in creation. *- The Tao Te Ching*

JESUS	KRISHNA
Following the will of his Father, He desired to lead all creation back to Him. *- Untitled Apocalypse*	Through the endless circles of time, all things revolve through Me. Yet I am not this action; I am the audience that watches the drama. *- The Bagavad Gita*
No one rules this One. He has no name…He looks to every side and sees only Himself. Being infinite, he cannot be comprehended. No likeness of Him exists. *- The Sophia of Jesus Christ*	That which I see on every side, limitless, with numerous mouths and eyes, and without beginning or end, is Lord of the universe. *- The Bagavad Gita*
Without fault and unchanging, He is blessed. No one knows Him for only He knows Himself. In him exists no imperfection. He is called Father of the universe. *- The Sophia of Jesus Christ*	Beyond all thought, more subtle than the subtlest is He, farther from the farthest, nearer than the nearest, He resides in the lotus heart of every being. *- Mundaka Upanishad*
God is Spirit, and those who worship him must worship in spirit and truth. *- The Gospel of John*	The power that pervades all action of nature and man is the power of God. To realize this is to become immortal. *- Kena Upanishad*

BUDDHA	LAO TZU
Universal Mind stores within it, all thoughts and all actions since the beginning of time. *- The Lankavatara Sutra*	It is the nature of all things to return to Tao. Tao gave birth to everything, yet nothing gave birth to it. *– The Tao Te Ching*
Essential Nature can be seen even by the novice, yet the novice does not recognize it. Seeing only in part, it is like he sees only one half of the universe. *- The Surangama Sutra*	It is a mystery. If you meet It, you cannot see Its face. If you follow It, you cannot see Its back. *– The Tao Te Ching*
There is no cessation of Divine Mind which, in itself, is the abode of Reality and the Womb of Truth. *- The Lankavatara Sutra*	People conform to earth. The earth follows the conventions of the sky; the sky emulates the Tao. The Tao conforms to its own nature. *– The Tao Te Ching*
Transcendental Intelligence is not subject to birth or death...it transcends all dualistic conceptions. *- The Lankavatara Sutra*	Tao is beyond all words. It can only be apprehended in silence. *– Chuang Tzu*

JESUS

He is limitless, for no one can set limits for Him. He is unfathomable, immeasurable, invisible, eternal, ineffable, and without name.
- *The Apocryphon of John*

The Father reaches out to those he loves so that those who have come from Him might also become Him.
- *The Tripartite Tractate*

That which you see is that which I revealed to you; but that which I Am, I alone know, and no one else. Allow me, then, this mystery which is My own, and that which is yours, behold it through Me. See me in truth that I Am—not what I said to you, but what you are able to know, for you are My family.
- *The Acts of John*

All things, all creatures, all forms exist within, and in relationship to, each other. They will eventually return to their essential nature.
- *The Gospel of Mary (Magdalene)*

KRISHNA

All the space between heaven and earth, and throughout the quarters of the universe, is filled with You alone.
- *The Bagavad Gita*

As countless sparks rise upward from the fire, so from the lowest point of the imperishable rises all things—to the depths do they return again…Through its own light the formless Being dwells within all and without all. It arises in all things and does not perish.
- *Mundaka Upanishad*

Intelligence, knowledge, illumination, patience, peace, happiness, misery, death, fear and fearlessness… all come from Me alone.
- *The Bagavad Gita*

As salt dissolves in water, we taste the water, but also the salt. Just so, the great Being which is without end or limit, and which consists only of Awareness, comes forth from such elements, and vanishes into them once more.
- *The Upanishads*

BUDDHA	LAO TZU
Universal Mind transcends all individuation and limits. Universal Mind is thoroughly pure in its essential nature, subsisting unchanged and free from faults of impermanence, undisturbed by egoism, unruffled by distinctions, desires and aversions. *- The Lankavatara Sutra*	Tao is like an empty bowl which can never be filled up. It cannot be measured but is the origin of all things…it unites the whole world. It resides in a hidden place, yet it exists forever. I do not know whose child it is. It seems to be the common ancestor of all, the father of things. *- The Tao Te Ching*
One intrinsic unity embraces all phenomena. *- The Surangma Sutra*	God does not answer with words. He does not call things, but they come. The great plan unfolds slowly, like a great net through which none are lost. *- The Tao Te Ching*
If anyone should say that the Great Buddha (Tathagata) comes or goes or sits or reclines, he fails to understand my teaching. Why? Because the Great Buddha has no where or when, therefore He is called Tathagata. *- The Diamond Sutra*	To name Tao is to name no-thing. Cause and chance have no influence on Tao. Tao is a name that indicates without defining. *- The Tao Te Ching*
Subtle influences cause things to appear, then disappear. Whether manifest or unmanifest, nothing exists in and by itself, but only in relationship to everything else. *- The Lankavatara Sutra*	Look, but you will not see it because it is without form. Try to listen to it, but it is soundless. Attempt to take hold of it. Impossible! It is without form. *- The Tao Te Ching*

"I sat there and forgot and forgot until what remained
was the river that went by, and I who watched.
Eventually the watcher joined the river, and there
was only one of us. I believe it was the river."

— Norman McLean

BEING ONE
Mind, Meditation and Yoga

"If the chimney is full of smoke,

how can the light be seen?

If the mind is full of dirt,

how can the soul shine?"

–Yogaswami

The goal of all mystical paths is to recognize oneness with God, or whatever one chooses to call Ultimate Reality. We are told by spiritual teachers that we already *are* One, we just don't realize it. In reality, there is nothing to achieve, nothing to become, nothing to do but...wake up! And to wake up, all we have to do is to clean our doors of perception, which will easily and automatically allow us to become aware of our essential unity with All-That-Is.

That's all we have to do, just this one thing. Yet only a handful of people in any age ever fully realize this ultimate state of awareness. And most of the few who have attained this state of being have done so only after a lifetime of arduous spiritual effort. We might well wonder, then, if we already *are* One, why is it so difficult to realize it?

In a sense, the answer to that question is in the very fact that we asked the question in the first place. We use our "rational" mind to seek an answer to something that can only be recognized by our super-rational mind. Our mind, it turns out, is both the problem and the solution.

While our rational mind can do many amazing things, and is very useful and necessary in the phenomenal world, when it comes to realizing God consciousness,

our thinking, questioning, debating, pondering mind gets us nowhere at all. All our mind does is steer us into a spiritual cul de sac.

But now that we've identified the problem, the solution seems pretty obvious and simple: just stop thinking—just power down our discursive mind so that "Essential Mind" can take over and, bingo, instant Buddha, instant Christ. If only!

The reality is that our minds are completely out of control. The human mind has often been compared to a hyper-active chattering monkey who refuses to stop moving or shut up. Anyone who has ever tried to meditate knows just how appropriate that metaphor is. Still, it would appear that we have no choice but to train our mind as if it were a new puppy that hasn't been housebroken yet. We need to become the master of our mind, not its slave.

JESUS	KRISHNA
Original Man had a single mind within him. *– The Dialogue of the Savior*	When the mind is not in harmony, this communion is not easy to attain. But someone whose mind is in harmony can attain it if he understands and works hard. *– Katha Upanishad*
Be aware of that which is right in front of you; then you will be able to grasp what is out of your sight. For there is nothing hidden that will not be known. *– The Gospel of Thomas*	The unreal never is. The Real never is not. Those possessed of this knowledge of Truth know both of these. *– The Bagavad Gita*
I (Mary Magdalene) saw the Lord in a vision and I said to him, "Lord, I saw you in a vision." He answered me, saying "You are blessed because your vision of Me did not falter. Where the mind is, there is your treasure." *– The Gospel of Mary (Magdalene)*	God, the Self which is hidden in all beings, is not revealed to all, but only to those who are wise and pure in heart, who concentrates the mind, He is then revealed. The senses of the wise person obey his mind. *– Katha Upanishad*
I said to Him, "Lord, what allows one to see a vision? Do we see it with the soul or with the spirit?" The Lord answered and said to me, "One sees not through the soul or the spirit, but through the Mind—which is between these two." *– The Gospel of Mary (Magdalene)*	When the mind is completely controlled in the practice of concentration, and when the Self is seen by the self, and when the yogi feels infinite bliss—which proceeds from the purified intellect and transcends the senses, that one never departs from his real state, and acquires nothing which is superior to this. *– The Bagavad Gita*

BUDDHA	LAO TZU
In the sky, there is no distinction of east and west; people create distinctions out of their own minds and then believe them to be true. *– The Buddha*	The grease that feeds the light devours itself. *– Chuang Tzu*
Do not dwell in the past, do not dream of the future, concentrate the mind on the present moment. *– The Buddha*	If you meet Tao you will not be able to see its face. If you follow Tao, you will not be able to see its back. But in embracing Tao, the present moment becomes obvious. *– The Tao Te Ching*
What we are today has come from yesterday's thoughts. Our present thoughts build our life of tomorrow: Our life is the creation of our mind. *– The Dhammapada*	Observe the simple; embrace what is essential. *– The Tao Te Ching*
The discriminating mind is a dance and a magician with the objective world as his stage. Intuitive-mind is the wise jester who travels with the magician and reflects upon his emptiness and transiency. *– The Lankavatara Sutra*	The one who speaks does not know. The one who knows does not speak. Close up the passageways. Blunt sharpness, untie tangles. Unite the world into one mystic whole… this is the highest good in the world. *– The Tao Te Ching*

JESUS	KRISHNA
It is the Mind that illuminates the body, so that when all things are in order within yourself, you will become luminous. *– The Dialogue of the Savior*	As a lamp sheltered from the wind, the yogi with a subdued mind who practices concentration in the Self, is like a lamp that does not flicker. *– The Bagavad Gita*
Unless one is born anew he will not be able to see the kingdom of God…unless one is born of water and the Spirit, he cannot enter the kingdom of God. That which is born of flesh is flesh. That which is born of spirit, spirit is. *– The Gospel of John*	All things born in truth must die, but out of death comes life. *– The Bagavad Gita*
It is a great vision when you see the Eternal One who alone Exists…Therefore, endeavor to keep for yourselves only those things that can follow you. Seek out that truth and speak from within It, so that everything within you is harmonious. For I tell you truly, the Living God is in you and you are in Him. *– The Dialogue of the Savior*	The one who does work for Me alone, who has Me as his highest goal, is devoted to Me, freed from attachment, and bearing no enmity toward any creature, that one comes to Me. *– The Bagavad Gita* He who sees Me in all things, and sees all things in Me, I dwell in him and he dwells in Me. *– The Bagavad Gita*
And when you pray, do not pray like the hypocrites do, out in public for everyone to see; but go into your inner chamber and shut the door, and pray to your Father in secret, and your Father in secret will reward you. *– The Gospel of Matthew*	Shutting out external objects; steadying the eyes between the eyebrows; restricting the even currents of Prana…the senses, mind and intellect controlled…free from desire, fear and anger: such a man of meditation is free forever. *– The Bagavad Gita*

BUDDHA	LAO TZU
If one speaks or acts with a pure mind, joy will follow, as if it was that person's own shadow. *– The Dhammapada*	In keeping the spirit and soul together, can you maintain their perfect harmony? *– The Tao Te Ching*
The cessation of the discriminating mind can not take place until there is a "turning-about" in the deepest seat of consciousness. *– The Lankavatara Scripture*	In gathering your vital energy so that you can create agility, have you achieved the state of a new-born child? In cleansing your inner vision, have you purified it of all dullness? *– The Tao Te Ching*
If and when the discriminating mind can be gotten rid of, the whole mind-system will cease to function and Universal Mind will alone remain. Getting rid of the discriminating mind removes the cause of all error. *– The Lankavatara Sutra*	The prudent embraces the One, and becomes the example for all those under Heaven. Not making a show of himself he is illuminated. Not justifying himself, he becomes acknowledged. Not boasting he receives credit. Not flaunting, he endures. Not competing, no one can compete with him. Bending, He becomes whole. Being whole, all things will come to him. *– The Tao Te Ching*
Meditate deeply. *– The Dhammapada*	Stop up your senses. Close the door. You will not be exhausted for as long as you live. *– The Tao Te Ching*

JESUS	KRISHNA
Become aware that I speak so that I may come forth. Focus attention on Me so that you may see Me! *– The Second Apocalypse of James*	With a serene heart, and without fear, being firm in one's vows, with his mind controlled, and thinking on Me, let him have Me for his supreme goal. *– The Bagavad Gita*
Find a place of stillness within yourself. *– The Gospel of Thomas*	With a quiet mind, silence and self harmony...with love in a heart that is pure, so is harmony of the mind. *– The Bagavad Gita*
As you see yourself in water or mirror, so see Me in yourselves. *– Agrapha*	See now...in this My body, the whole universe centered in One... *– The Bagavad Gita*
I came from the great Power to those who meditate upon Me. I have been found in those who seek Me. See Me. Consider Me. Hear Me, you who have ears to hear. *- The Thunder: Perfect Mind*	He who is content and meditative, controlling the passions, and filled with firm resolve, with mind and heart centered on Me, He who is thus consecrated to Me is dear to Me. *– The Bagavad Gita*
Whoever drinks from my mouth will be as I am, and I will become him. And everything that is hidden will be revealed to him. *– The Gospel of Thomas*	At all times, remember Me...with mind and intellect absorbed in Me, you will doubtless come to Me. *The Bagavad Gita*

BUDDHA	LAO TZU
If you meditate in earnest, with a pure mind and kind deeds, leading a life with discipline and harmony with the dharma, you will grow in glory. If you meditate in earnest, and have spiritual discipline, you can create an island for yourself that even floodwaters cannot overwhelm. – *The Dhammapada*	The wise set their hearts upon the essence rather than what surrounds it. They choose the fruit, not the flower, and they prefer what is within to what is without. – *The Tao Te Ching*
The subject is quieted when the object ceases. The object ceases when the subject is quieted. – *The Manual on Zen Buddhism*	Realize ultimate emptiness. Achieve interior peace. Be steady in stillness. – *The Tao Te Ching*
As sentient beings wish to return to their origin where there is perfect unity, there are many expedient ways for doing so. – *The Surangama Sutra*	Once you grasp the Essence behind the essence, you are free to act beyond evil and fear. Then you will be at peace with yourself. – *The Tao Te Ching*
To reach the other shore of existence you must give up what is before you, behind you and between. Free your mind, transcend birth and death. – *The Dhammapada*	As I walk the path of Tao I become ignorant of all else. I fear only that I go astray. The Way is great, straight and smooth, yet others prefer smaller paths. – *The Tao Te Ching*
Drink the nectar of the dharma from within the depths of meditation, and free yourselves from both sin and fear. – *The Dhammapada*	With minds free and thoughts gone, the countenance becomes clear and serene. – *The Tao Te Ching*

JESUS	KRISHNA
You who have waited for Me, receive Me in yourself. Do not cast me away from you. Do not speak against Me with your voice, or remove Me from your hearing. Do not be in ignorance of Me at any time or in any place. Guard yourselves and do not be ignorant of Me. – *The Thunder: Perfect Mind*	He who sees Me in all things, and sees all things in Me, he never becomes separated from Me, nor do I become separated from him. The one who has attained unity worships Me, who dwells in all beings. Whatever his station in life, the yogi abides in Me. – *The Bagavad Gita*
Blessed are the solitary, and those who have been chosen. For they will find the kingdom. – *The Gospel of Thomas*	When the completely controlled mind rests serenely in the Self alone, free from longing after all desires, then it is one called steadfast in the Self. – *The Bagavad Gita*
Recognize your Self in Me who am speaking. Recognize My actions and keep My mysteries in silence. – *The Hymn of Jesus from The Acts of John*	With the mind focused on Me, taking refuge in Me, and practicing yoga, know that you will without doubt know Me fully. – *The Bagavad Gita*
When you make the two one, you will become the children of true humanity, and you will say to the mountain, "Move," and it will move. – *The Gospel of Thomas*	Where the channels are brought together like the spokes of a wheel, there He moves about, revealing Himself. Meditate, then, on Him, and cross over the farthest shore, beyond the darkness. – *The Upanishads*

BUDDHA	LAO TZU

Sitting alone, sleeping alone, going about alone, vanquish the ego by yourself alone. Abiding joy will be yours when all selfish desires end. – *The Dhammapada*	Though there may be many beautiful sights to see, one achieves peace by staying at home. – *The Tao Te Ching*
Those who meditate and keep their senses under control are able to do always what ought to be done…and, so, their suffering ceases. – *The Dhammapada*	The way of Tao is return. From its weakness comes its usefulness. All things come from that which exists, but that which exists comes from nothing. – *The Tao Te Ching*
Those who follow the dharma well taught reach the other shore…so hard to reach. But those who cross are beyond the power of death. – *The Dhammapada*	To be one with Tao is to live in Eternity. There is safety and wholeness there—even after death. – *The Tao Te Ching*

JESUS	KRISHNA
Come to Me because my yoke (yoga) is easy and my lordship gentle, and you will find peace for yourselves. – *The Gospel of Thomas*	Supreme bliss comes to the yogi with a tranquil mind, with his passions subdued, with the mind absorbed in God, the yogi is free from any stain. – *The Bagavad Gita*
I will reveal all things, beloved so that through knowledge and understanding you will become like Me. I will reveal the hidden things to you. Now put forth your hands and grasp Me... – *The Second Apocalypse of James*	Putting intelligence aside, and with the mind concentrated on the Self, the yogi will attain a state of quietness in stages. Let him not think on anything. – *The Bagavad Gita*

BUDDHA	LAO TZU

Come and follow...plunge into the incomparable
bliss of the spiritual life and abide in it.
– The Anguttara Nikaya

Fish need to get lost in water. People
need to get lost in Tao.
– Chuang Tzu

Be energetic in attaining what has yet to be attained,
master what has yet to be mastered, realize what has yet
to be realized...so that your spiritual life may bear
fruit, and you may continue to grow.
– The Samyutta Nikaya

How do I know the world? By that which is within me.
– The Tao Te Ching

"When you touch one thing with deep awareness, you touch everything. When the mind is quiet, all is Self. When the mind moves, the world arises. So be still. Throw away everything and be free."

– *Papaji*

THE SELF

"How shall I grasp it? Do not grasp it.
That which remains when there is
no more grasping is the Self."

– *Panchadasi*

When most of us use the word, "self," we are usually referring to our ego identity—that persona, or mask, we wear to maintain our illusion of individuality. This small self includes our subconscious mind, our intuitive mind, and virtually everything else our brains produce that make us believe that we are separate and apart from every other thing in the Universe.

Krishna, Plato and Jesus, however, meant something entirely different when they used this word "self." Self, to them, refers to what lies beneath individuality. This Self is the core essence of what (not who) we really are: God, the Tao, Universal Mind. Self is what remains when the little self dies. Self is what we discover when we are "born again." Self is what appears when we cleanse our windows of perception. Self is what we recognize when we "wake up." Self, really, is all that exists.

This Self, in Hinduism, is called "Atman." And Atman, Krishna tells us in The Bagavad Gita, is Brahman, or God. The only distinction between Atman and Brahman—between Self and God—is the distinction we make ourselves. Remove that distinction and all that remains is God, or Universal Mind, or Tao.

Gnostics often referred to Self as a "spark," and God as the divine Light from which the spark emanated. For them, individual sparks of divine Light had broken off from the Godhead, and were trapped within, and by, the human body. In our ignorance, humans are unaware that this spark of Light exists within us. But when we become aware of our true nature, the Self, we dissolve back into the Divine Light.

Unlike Hindus and Gnostic-Christians, Buddhists rarely speak of Self in the same way Jesus and Krishna do. In fact, much Buddhist teaching emphasizes "not-Self." Although pursuing much the same course toward enlightenment, the Buddha often turned the mind back on itself through the process of negation: "not this, not that." This process forces the disciple to give up all thought patterns by exhausting them, as in Zen Buddhist training. The closest concept to Self in Buddhism is "Mind"—not the intellectual mind, but what stands behind it. Inasmuch as there is a section in the book on Mind, we will leave these teachings for later.

Neither did ancient Taoism emphasize the concept of Self. While not denying it, Taoists of old simply emphasized the reality of Tao alone. Perhaps the Taoist masters decided that giving name to something other than Tao would be too misleading, and give rise to too much philosophy. After all, when one's sense of individuality disappears, there is nothing left but Tao. Buddhists might add the comment that that ego is an illusion, and Tao was all that ever existed in the first place.

But what precipitates the ego's disappearance? What causes the thinking mind to cease its thinking? Lao Tzu might say that any attempt to answer such questions would require too much activity of the discriminating mind. Better to just shrug one's shoulders and laugh.

JESUS	KRISHNA
If you have come to know yourSelf, then you will be called the one who knows himSelf. But if you do not know yourSelf, then you know nothing. But for those who have known themSelves, also know the All. – *The Book of Thomas the Contender*	The yogis who strive for perfection see the Self dwelling in themselves; but those who do not strive and are not intelligent, are unaware of Self. – *The Bagavad Gita*
He who sees himself only on the outside, not within, becomes small and makes others small. – *The Gospel of Mani*	The Self is hidden in all beings, but is manifest only to those who have the intuitive abilities to recognize it. – *The Upanishads*
Everyone who has known the Self within, sees it in everything he does. – *Dialogue of the Savior*	He who devotes himself only to the Self within, and holds it dear—the object of his devotion will never perish. – *The Upanishads*
You recognized Spirit and became Spirit. You saw Christ, and you became Christ. You saw the Father and you will become the Father. And yet, if you do not recognize these things as your Self, you will not become what you see. But if you recognize your Self, that which you see, you will become. – *The Gospel of Philip*	Seeing the Lord equally, everywhere, one does not injure the Self by the self, and so goes to his reward. – *The Bagavad Gita*

BUDDHA	LAO TZU

He who knows others is wise. He who knows himSelf is enlightened.
– *The Tao Te Ching*

Some see the Self as wondrous. Others speak of It as marvelous. Others hear of It and wonder. Still others hear of It, but do not understand It at all.
– *The Tao Te Ching*

He who experiences the unity of life sees his own Self in all beings, and all beings in his own Self, and looks on everything with an impartial eye.
– *The Buddha*

What is more important, recognition or the Self?...The Self which is restrained will not suffer, but endures forever.
– *The Tao Te Ching*

JESUS	KRISHNA
That which you have will save you if you bring it forth from yourselves. That which you do not have within you will kill you if you do not recognize it within you. – *The Gospel of Thomas*	Things in life are not valued so that we love them, but that we may love the Self through all things. – *The Upanishads*
The Kingdom exists within you, and outside of you. When you come to know yourSelves you will be known, and you will understand that you are children of the living Father. – *The Gospel of Thomas*	The wise, through meditation on the Self, recognizes the Ancient—who is difficult to see—enters the darkness for that which is hidden in a cave, and dwells in the abyss as God. This one leaves joy and sorrow far behind. – *The Upanishads*
Strive to know yourSelves. Become aware that you are children of the living Father; and you will know that you are living in the City of God, and you are that City. – *Oxyrhynchus fragment*	When one sees the separate existence of beings inherent in the One, he becomes God. – *The Bagavad Gita*
Strive to save those things that can follow you. Seek it, and speak from within it, so that everything you seek is in harmony within you. For I tell you truly, the living God dwells within you, and you in Him. – *Dialogue of the Savior*	Without beginning, and absent of qualities, the supreme Self is immutable... Though it exists in the body, it does not act, and cannot be affected. – *The Bagavad Gita*

BUDDHA	LAO TZU

Of that which is transient and subject to suffering and change, one cannot rightly say: "This belongs to me; this am I; this is my Self.
– *The Buddha*

The man of Tao remains unknown. In perfect virtue, he produces nothing. "No Self" is "true Self." And the greatest man is Nobody.
– *Chuang Tzu*

JESUS	KRISHNA
Judas said, "Tell us what existed before heaven and earth came into being." The Lord said, "There was darkness, and water, and the Spirit upon the water. Yet I tell you truly that what you are seeking is already within you…" – *Dialogue of the Savior*	The Self, the very smallest thing is greater than the greatest thing. It resides in the heart of every being. He who no longer has desires or grief, sees the splendor of the Self through the grace of God. – *The Upanishads*
Truly, the living God dwells within you, and you in Him. – *Dialogue of the Savior*	When one sees all beings in the Self, and the Self in all beings, he hates no one. – *Isha Upanishad*
I Am that which cannot be measured or known, but I reveal Myself as I wish…I am the All, since I exist in everyone. – *Trimorphic Protennoia*	The Self of knowledge is unborn, and never dies. It proceeds out of nothing, and nothing proceeds from it. That which is unborn and eternal cannot be killed even when the body is killed. – *The Upanishads*
That which you seek is within you… – *Dialogue of the Savior*	When the Self is one's only wish, wishes are fulfilled— and one becomes free from sorrow. – *The Upanishads*

"I Am that I Am."

– Exodus 3:14

THE SACRED SYLLABLE

In the Presence of the Avatar

*"OM (AUM) is not an immaterial abstraction
which transcends the world of matter and earthly
existence; it is the world we live in but do not see. It is
here—now, I-Thou, and 'the reality that flows.'"*

– *William Braden*

One of the truly amazing parallels between Christian and Hindu texts is the use of the phrase, "I Am." The author of the canonical Gospel of John has Jesus use these words quite often when referring to himself as the incarnation of God. Orthodox Christians took such phrases as "I and the Father are one," literally. Rather than understanding the statement in a mystical sense, they believed that Jesus, and no one else, could identify with God the Father.

Gnostic-Christians, however, used the phrase "I Am" in its original, mystical, context. The Jesus who speaks these words in the Gnostic Gospels is not the historical teacher from Galilee; he is the eternal Christ, the avatar—the incarnation—of the Godhead who takes on human form again and again throughout human history. The Hindu avatar, Krishna, uses the phrase in precisely the same way. In fact, as the reader will discover, the "I Am" statements in both the Bagavad Gita and the Gnostic-Gospels are so similar in language and content that they are essentially interchangeable. In these texts, Krishna and Christ are transparent beings who channel the voice of God.

The use of the term, "I Am" is also familiar to every Jew. In the Hebrew Bible, these words are the "name" of God: "Yahweh," which is variously translated as "I Am," "I Am that I Am," or "He who Is." The word, Yahweh, is related to the Hebrew verb "to be," but goes beyond that sense to suggest the active presence. It implies that God is immanent in our lives.

This "active presence" word for God, however, did not originate with the Jews. As a name for God, it was well known among all Semitic peoples long before the advent of monotheism. It is possible that ancestors of the Hebrews picked up the term during their sojourn as slaves in Egypt. The tribe of Levi, to which Moses belonged, knew the word and knew that it was often used in a shortened form— Yo! Yah! or Yahu!—as a mantra.

Both the ancient Egyptian priests and the Brahmins of India understood the fundamental principles of vibrotherapeutics. Both those religions used sacred syllables as chants and mantras to set up vibratory reactions which were useful for healing. Their toning was also used to stimulate latent centers of human consciousness.

For the ancient Brahmins, as well as for modern Hindus, the sacred syllable, AUM, represents the primal sound of creation. It is considered to be the "hum" of the Universe. Is it possible that there is a linguistic connection between the sacred Hindu syllable, AUM, and the Semitic name for God? Even the English "I Am" sounds much like the Sanskrit "AUM." Whatever the case, linguistically, both avatars of God, Christ and Krishna, incorporate the essence of Being-ness in their use of the expression "I Am."

JESUS	KRISHNA
I Am the Light which shines everywhere. I Am the All. All things have gone forth from Me, and all things shall return to Me. Cleave the wood and I Am there. Turn the stone, and you will find Me. *- The Gospel of Thomas*	I Am the origin of all things. All things proceed from Me. I Am the source of all beings, and all beings exist within Me. No being, whether moving or unmoving, can exist without Me. *- The Bagavad Gita*
I am All and All. I am the Father, the Mother, the Son. All that moves, moves in Me. All that exists, exists in Me. I Am the womb that gives life to all creatures. I Am the invisible one that exists within the All. *- Trimorphic Protennoia*	I Am the Father of the Universe. I Am the Source of the Father. I Am the Mother of the Universe. I Am the creator of all things. I Am the highest of all things known, the Way of purification, the sacred syllable, AUM. *- The Bagavad Gita*
I dwell in every soul. I awaken those who sleep. My voice cries out in those who love Me. I existed before the beginning. *- Trimorphic Protennoia*	I Am the Self which exists in the heart of every being. I Am the beginning, the middle, and the end of all things. *- The Bagavad Gita*
I Am revealed to those who love Me. I dwell in silence, and I Am a voice that cries out in those who seek me. *- Trimorphic Protennoia*	I Am the soul which dwells in the heart of all that exists. I Am the beginning. I Am the middle. I Am the end of all things which have life. *- The Bagavad Gita*

JESUS	KRISHNA
I am the One who dwells within you. I Am the Father. I Am the Mother. I Am the Son. I Am the One who is beyond corruption. I Am the seed that is planted within every being. *- The Apocryphon of John*	I am the Father of the Universe. I am the Mother. I sustain all beings. I am the Way, the Supporter, the Lord, the Witness, the Abode, the Refuge, the Friend, the Origin and the Dissolution, the resting place, and the ground which holds the eternal seed. *- The Bagavad Gita*
I Am you, and you are Me, and where you are, there I Am. I Am sown in all things, and when you gather Me, it is you, yourself, whom you gather. *- The Gospel of Eve*	I Am the same to all beings; my love is equal for all. Through devotion, those who worship Me are in Me, and I Am in them. *- The Bagavad Gita*
I Am in everything. I uphold the heavens. I Am the foundation which supports the planets. I Am the Light that shines everywhere, that gives joy to souls. *- Manichean psalm*	I Am the sweet fragrance in earth, the life of all beings and the austerity in ascetics. *- The Bagavad Gita*
I Am the life of the world: I Am the sap in trees, and the sweet water that lies beneath the children of matter. *- Manichean psalm*	I Am the wetness in water...I Am the radiance in the moon and the sun. I Am the Om in the Vedas. The manhood in men Am I. *- The Bagavad Gita*
I Am the bread of life; he who comes to Me shall not hunger, and he who believes in Me shall never thirst. *- The Gospel of John*	I Am easily attainable by the devoted yogi who keeps his mind on Me, who remembers Me with a singleness of purpose. *- The Bagavad Gita*

JESUS	KRISHNA
I Am the first Thought that dwells in the Light. I Am the movement that dwells in the All. I Am She in whom the All manifests. I Am the invisible and the revealed. I cannot be measured. No words can describe me. Yet I can be known within the silence of the One. I move in all things. *- Trimorphic Protennoia*	I Am Time which cannot be exhausted. I Am the sustainer of all that has been formed. I Am the all seizing death...the prosperity of those who are prosperous. I Am fame, beauty, inspiration, memory, intelligence, and that which always remains. Of the hidden mysteries, I Am silence. And of those who know, I Am knowledge. *- The Bagavad Gita*
I can be heard in everything. I Am the speech that cannot be grasped. I alone exist. *- The Thunder: Perfect Mind*	Know Me as the eternal seed of all beings, the intellect of the intelligence, and heroism of the hero. *- The Bagavad Gita*
I Am the first begotten one. I Am the beloved. I am the one alone who is righteous. I speak out so that you may hear Me. Attend to Me so that you may see Me. *- The (Second) Apocalypse of James*	Although I Am unborn, everlasting, and I Am the Lord of all. I come to my realm of nature and through my wondrous power I am born. I Am OM, the eternal Word. I Am the silent prayer. *- The Bagavad Gita*
I Am a mirror to all who see Me. Me; a door for all who knock upon Me. I Am your couch—rest yourself upon Me. *- The Hymn of Christ from the Acts of John*	I Am the Way, the Master who watches in silence; I Am your friend. I Am your shelter. I Am your dwelling place of peace. *- The Bagavad Gita*
I Am as near to you as the clothing of your body. *- Coptic psalm book*	I pervade all that exists in my unmanifested form. All beings exist in Me. *- The Bagavad Gita*

JESUS	KRISHNA
I Am the perfect thought of the Invisible One. Through Me the All became manifest. I Am the Mother and the Light. *- Trimorphic Protennoia*	I Am the knowledge of the soul, time that does not end, the Creator who sees all. I Am death that carries away all things, and I Am the Source of all things that will come to be. *- The Bagavad Gita*
I Am a Lamp that you might see Me. I Am a mirror so that you may know Me. I Am a door so that you may knock upon Me. I Am a Path for you who travel. *- The Hymn of Jesus, from the Acts of John*	Through mercy I abide in the hearts of those who worship me. I dispel the darkness of ignorance through the light of wisdom. *- The Bagavad Gita*
I Am the beginning and the end. I Am the one who is honored and the one who is despised. I Am the holy one and the whore. I Am the virgin and the wife. I Am the one without children and many are my sons. *- The Thunder: Perfect Mind*	I Am the beginning, the middle, and the end. I Am the sacrifice and I Am the offering. I Am the holy gift and the holy plant. I Am sacred foods, sacred words, and the holy fire into which the offering is made. *- The Bagavad Gita*
I Am the living One, the Father who will reveal to you all that is hidden, that through understanding you will become as I Am. Reach forth your hand and take hold of Me. *- The (Second) Apocalypse of James*	I Am the Father of this world, the Mother, the Sustainer, the Grandfather, the Purifier, the One thing to be known. *- The Bagavad Gita*
I Am the One who exists in kingdom of the Undivided. *- The Gospel of Thomas*	Know that with merest fraction of my Being I pervade the Universe. Know that I Am. *- The Bagavad Gita*

"When you don't require anything from the world, and nothing from God—when you don't desire anything, when you don't strive for anything, when you don't expect anything, the divine will enter you, unmasked and unexpected."

– Nisargadatta

CUTTING THE TIES THAT BIND

The Path of Renunciation

"Do not be afraid. I am rich.
I will fill you with my wealth."

– *The Gospel of the Savior*

One of my spiritual heroes is Mahatma Gandhi. History records his heroic exploits in freeing India from British rule and vastly improving the lot of the Indian people. Many people are familiar with Gandhi's lasting model for non-violent civil disobedience. Like Jesus, the Mahatma was a living example of ahimsa, or non-violence, in the face of oppression. And, like Jesus, Gandhi not only turned his own cheek, but taught his people the value of overcoming violence and hate with peace and love.

For Gandhi, the search for truth required that he follow the path of renunciation—being in the world, without being of it. The practical application of renunciation was, for Gandhi, and all others who have ever taken such vows, to strip away virtually everything in life that stands between oneself and God. While much of Gandhi's autobiography is devoted to the actions and events of his life on the world stage, it also chronicles his journey of self-conquest through gradual transformation.

The Mahatma was born Mohandas K. Gandhi in Porbandar, India, in 1869. His family was one of privilege, and his young life was one of ease and comfort. At the tender age of thirteen, Gandhi married his life-long wife, Kasturbai. As a young adult he took up the practice of law, and looked forward to a life as a typical and successful member of the middle class, with all the materialism such a life implies.

Then Gandhi's life began to change. By the time he was assassinated many years later, the Mahatma owned only seven possessions: his spectacles, his begging bowl, his loin cloth, his sandals, and one copy each of The Bible, The Bagavad Gita, and The Koran.

Sitting at the feet of my own guru from India (Eknath Easwaran) during the 1960s, I loved to hear him tell stories about the Mahatma (Great Soul), whom he had met as a child. One such story had to do with Gandhi's attendance at summit meetings with other world leaders: Joseph Stalin, Franklin D. Roosevelt and Winston Churchill. Gandhi was deeply bothered by both the smoke and smell of cigars, so whenever he attended a summit he would intentionally seat himself next to Winston Churchill, just so he could light his cigars for him. By these physical acts, Gandhi conquered his aversion to smoke, and practiced compassion at the same time.

Another favorite story is about a mother who came to Gandhi one day, with her young son in tow. "Gandhiji," she pleaded, "please tell my son to stop eating sugar." Gandhi told her, "Come back in three days." Puzzled, the mother did as she was asked and went back home. When she returned with her son three days later, Gandhi told the boy, "Stop eating sugar." The mother then asked Gandhi, "Why didn't you just tell him to stop eating sugar three days ago?" "Because," the Mahatma said, "three days ago I hadn't stopped eating sugar myself."

Inevitably, the day arrived in his married life when Gandhi decided it was time to let go of sex and take a vow of celibacy. His long-suffering wife, Kasturbai, was not at all pleased by this decision, but she understood her husband's purpose in taking this vow. Difficult as it was for her, Kasturbai always supported her husband's feats of spiritual athleticism in the end.

What Gandhi practiced in life, he practiced in the act of dying as well. Eknath Easwaran, in his book, *Gandhi the Man*, describes the last moments of the last day in Gandhiji's life:

> Gandhi was in Delhi, consuming every waking moment in a last plea for Hindu-Muslim unity. When it came time for the prayer meeting he walked to it briskly, as he always did, with his arms on the shoulders of two of the ashram girls. A dense crowd had gathered to hear him speak. As he walked to the platform through the crowd, Gandhi held his palms together in front of him in greeting. As he did so, a young man blinded with hatred placed himself in Gandhi's path, greeted him with the same gesture of his hands, and fired a gun point-blank into Gandhi's heart. Such is the greatness of this little man's love that as his body fell, nothing but the mantram which was deep within him came to his lips, Rama, Rama, Rama. It meant I forgive you, I love you, I bless you.

Saint Francis of Assisi renounced the world in a slightly different way. The story goes that Francis, being born into a wealthy family like the historical Buddha, one day had

a mystical experience of God that immediately changed his life and the way he looked at material possessions and social status. Unlike Gandhi, who let worldly things drop away one at a time, Saint Francis was said to have taken all of his possessions, including the clothes he was wearing, and thrown them out the window of his father's house, into the eager arms of those less fortunate. Then Francis, quite naked, walked out the front door and never looked back. From that moment on, Francis devoted every moment of his life to the service of God through his service to the sick, the poor and the outcast.

The path of renunciation has never been a popular path for the vast majority of the human race, and it is especially unpopular for those of us who live in a culture that worships power, possessions and pleasure above all else. For Christians—outside of Catholic monastic traditions—Jesus' clear call to leave the world in favor of the kingdom of God has been pretty much ignored.

Nevertheless, Jesus, Krishna, the Buddha and Lao Tzu all considered renunciation a necessary part of the spiritual path that cannot be avoided if one wishes to achieve enlightenment in this lifetime. But the path of the renunciate is a path that only a few will ever take in any age. Such a journey is even harder to contemplate for those of us who live in a materialistic culture that places little value on spiritual pursuits.

Neither do we have any cultural models. There may be Catholic monasteries and nunneries where voluntary poverty and celibacy is practiced, but even these few models are safely hidden away. We don't have the benefit of living in a spiritually-oriented culture where temples, wandering sadhus, monks and nuns with shaved heads and begging bowls, are integral parts of the social fabric. In our culture, poverty is usually seen as failure, and celibacy is only practiced by pre-teens.

But every once in awhile we might catch a glimpse of what it really means to devote one's entire life to God, and to nothing else. For me, the clearest memories of what it means to become a renunciate come from the 1960s and '70s when I was young, didn't own much anyway, and had taken up the hippie lifestyle—which had a natural disdain for all things material.

After graduating from seminary in 1970, I was ordained by The American Lutheran Church, and became the national Church's one and only pastor to the "Counter Culture." I didn't exactly look like a Lutheran pastor—not with my long hair, beads, bells, bellbottoms and bare feet—so the Church really didn't know what to make of me. The bishop, the pastors and the laity supposed I looked the way I did so that I could better minister to young people. And I didn't try to convince them otherwise.

The focus of my ministry was a halfway house I opened to take in young people with a variety of problems: teenagers, as well as young men and women who needed counseling and emotional support as much as they needed food and shelter.

The national office of the Church funded the ministry to the

extent that it paid for the facility and my meager salary. With no allocation for food, I had to raise money outside of the Church, but I was never able to generate enough money to pay for the staff I badly needed. However, I could offer volunteers room and board in exchange for time and talent. For young people back then, food and shelter was often more than enough. Voluntary poverty for the Counter Culture was actually a source of pride—being both a spiritual lifestyle, and a political statement.

Our very first volunteer was a young man who did the cooking for the household. David was twenty-two years old, and had a very gentle soul. His warmth seemed to be generated by the energy of light alone.

All of us loved David, which is why we were all very happy for him when, after a number of months with us, he met the girl of his dreams and asked her to marry him. Even though this meant he would be leaving us to live with his new bride, we wished David all the happiness in the world.

David was also a very handsome young man, and his fiance was both a wonderful person and quite beautiful. The pair were a storybook couple, and we thought of them as a fairy tale prince and princess who would live happily ever after.

Finally the wedding day rolled around, and I performed the simple ceremony. We all kissed the bride, congratulated the groom, and threw rice as David and his princess got into their carriage and headed off on their honeymoon.

The trouble with fairy tales is that they don't always have

happy endings. As the newly married couple were driving down the Big Sur coast—with its narrow two lanes and hairpin curves, high above the roiling sea—something happened that caused David's car to veer off the road. It crashed through the barriers at the edge of the perilous cliffs and became airborne. We never learned what caused the accident, or exactly what had happened. All we knew for sure was that David and his beautiful bride plunged a thousand feet to their deaths—on the happiest day of their lives.

We were still grieving for these young people the day Steven came to us. Like David, he had no possessions other than the clothes on his back. And no shoes. Stephen had stopped wearing shoes years before, he told us, because—if you wear shoes, the whole earth is covered with leather (or rubber or whatever.) The point being that you can't truly feel the Earth unless you walk with bare feet.

Steven, like David, was an especially gentle soul, and all of us quickly came to see him as a sadhu, a wandering holy man. Steven's words were soft and kind, but the major influence he had on the household was due to the example he set. Steve was a vegetarian, so the house became vegetarian. Steven wore no shoes, so we took off ours. Now we could actually feel Mother Earth supporting us.

Once a week my wife would go to the supermarket with fifty dollars—all that we could afford to feed a dozen people for a week—and a general shopping list from Steven. From this, Steve provided three meals a day, seven days a week, using just what we had available, and none of us ever went hungry.

As a spiritual discipline, Steven fasted one day a week, so several of us started fasting one day a week as well. Twice a year—the week before Christmas and the week before Easter, Steven would fast for seven straight days. He prepared a feast on Christmas day, and again on Easter Sunday. He served dinner and sat down with us, sharing grace and our company. And while the rest of us stuffed ourselves like turkeys, Steven maintained his fast.

Although Steve never bought anything for himself, he encouraged me to buy—for the house—all seven albums by the Moody Blues. He then turned us on to the profound spiritual message in these recordings, and we probably listened to every album—Steve's Bible—a thousand times.

One day, after several years had passed, Steven announced that it was time for him to move on. He said his goodbyes, and we all had tears in our eyes as we hugged him. Then the young sadhu turned and walked out of our lives forever. He left with just the clothes on his back, and no shoes.

Steve was a rare example of what it means to be a spiritual "athlete." He was a hero in that he had succeeded in conquering himself. Most of us, at least in this lifetime, won't become renunciates. But we can gain inspiration and strength from hearing the stories, and reading the words, of those who have.

———————————

Eknath Easwaran, Gandhi the Man, Glide Publications, San Francisco, 1972, p. 140.

JESUS	KRISHNA
There was a man of great wealth who said to himself: "I will fill my storehouses with all my produce, and then I will be secure." This is what the man thought, but that very night he died. Those who have ears to hear, should hear. *- The Gospel of Thomas*	People think that all that they have gained is theirs. They will boast of their wealth, and revel in it. But those who are addicted to the gratification of the senses will fall into a foul hell. *- The Bagavad Gita*
Sending out his disciples, Jesus said, "Take no gold, nor silver, nor copper in your belts, no bag for your journey, nor two tunics, nor sandals, nor a staff; for the laborer deserves his food. *- The Gospels of Matthew, Mark and Luke*	
Do not accumulate earthly possessions, which moths and rust can destroy, and which robbers can steal. Rather, store up heavenly treasures which cannot be destroyed or stolen. For wherever your heart is, there is your treasure as well. *- The Gospels of Matthew, Luke and Thomas*	The desire for wealth can never bring happiness. If wealth is acquired, there is great anxiety in the effort to keep it. If it is lost, the loss is felt as if it were death…Even if one acquires and retains wealth, the person of wealth is not satisfied, but continues to seek more. Wealth only increases one's desire. *- Santiparva Mahabharata*
It is easier for a camel to go through the eye of a needle than for a rich man to enter the kingdom of God. *- The Gospels of Matthew, Mark and Luke*	Those who rejoice in the Self become masters of themselves, and the master of all worlds. Those who do not know this truth are slaves. *Chandogya Upanishad*

BUDDHA	LAO TZU
People suppose that their wealth and families belong to them. But nothing belongs to us, and having such thoughts only leads to suffering. *- The Dhammapada*	Jade, gold, wealth, power, pride—these things bestow their own doom. *- The Tao Te Ching*
Like a bird which is content wherever it goes—its wings its only burden, the monk is content with one set of robes, and a bowl for his daily food. Wherever he goes, he takes only the bare necessities. *- The Kevaddha Sutta*	The sage moves through life not caring about home or name, living simply. Lacking distinction, others think him a fool. But he judges no one. His feet leave no prints. This is the perfect man. His boat is empty. *- Chuang Tzu*
One buries treasure believing that there will be need of it in the future... But acting with charity and goodness, the self-controlled man stores up hidden treasure no thief can steal. *- Khuddaka Patha*	No peace comes to a wealthy man, even if he owns mansions filled with gold and jewels. He must then guard his treasure against those who would steal it. Destruction follows such people. *- The Tao Te Ching*
One road leads to wealth, the other to Nirvana. Knowing this, the monk will seek to separate himself from the world. *- The Dhammapada*	Those who are so concerned with their lives make life unbearable for themselves. Even when they have what they want, they are not happy. They want to accumulate even more. *- Chuang Tzu*

JESUS	KRISHNA
For what does it profit a man if he gains the whole world and loses his own soul? *- The Gospel of the Egyptians, Matthew, Mark, Luke and John*	Those ruined souls and small intellects become the enemies of the world and are filled with insatiable desires. *- The Bagavad Gita*
For those who seek those things that this life offers, that is their wealth. But the pleasures of this world are false, and its gold and its silver have no substance. *- Dialogue of the Savior*	All the wealth one earns is transitory...so those who die without having realized the Self and its right desires finds no permanent happiness in any world to which they go. *- Chandogya Upanishad*
Go and sell what you have, and give it to the poor; then you will have riches in heaven. *- The Gospel of Mark*	Eternity will not appear to those who are deluded by the illusion of wealth. *- The Upanishads*

No one can serve two masters; for either he will hate the one and love the other, or he will be devoted to the one and despise the other. You cannot serve both God and wealth.
- The Gospels of Thomas, Matthew and Luke

The Kingdom of the Father is like a businessman who found among his inventory, a pearl. Being wise, the businessman kept the pearl and sold all the rest. You, too, must seek the treasures that endure, those which do not perish, and which neither moth nor worm can destroy.
- The Gospels of Thomas and Matthew

BUDDHA	LAO TZU
Right resolves are the resolve to renounce the world and to do no hurt or harm. *- Majjhima-Nikaya*	The person who lets the things of the world control him, loses possession of his inner self. *- Chuang Tzu*
The man of virtue abstains from accepting gold and money. *- The Kevaddha Sutta*	The wise person leaves the gold buried in the mountains and lets the pearl remain in the deep. *- Chang Tzu*
The circumstances that set up the conditions for re-birth are those which have to do with cravings for sensual pleasures. *- Majjhima-nikaya*	The person who gives from his abundance to those in need lives according to the Way. *- Tao Te Ching*
Men who are tied to their families and possessions are more helpless than those who are in prison. When there is an occasion for the prisoner to be released, the householder has no desire to leave his burdens. *- The Tevigga Sutta*	Which is more precious: fame or life? What has more value: riches or life? What gives one the most trouble: gain or loss? One naturally seeks after those things he most prizes. Therefore one must be careful about prizing the right things. *- The Tao Te Ching*

JESUS	KRISHNA
Woe to you who allow the body to rule over you. Putting your trust in the world, the world has become your god. You are destroying your souls with the desires that burn within you. *- The Book of Thomas the Contender*	Filled with insatiable desires, overcome by immense cares, bound by the ties of wealth and lust for sensual pleasure, all such burdens lead to death and the miseries of hell. *- The Bagavad Gita*
Beware of the desire for things, for one's life does not equal an abundance of possessions. *- The Gospel of Luke*	That which most people treasure is transient and fleeting, but eternity cannot be attained through things that are not eternal. *- The Upanishads*
Seek that which is great, and the little things will be given you; seek for heavenly things, and the earthly will be added to you. *- Agrapha*	
Anyone who forsakes family and possessions, and willingly takes up his cross and follows Me, will receive everything I have promised. And I will reveal to him the hidden mysteries. *- Untitled Apocalypse and The Gospels of Thomas, Matthew and Luke*	When all desires of the heart cease, then a person who is mortal becomes immortal and obtains God. When the ties of the heart are severed here on earth, then the mortal becomes immortal. *- The Upanishads*

BUDDHA	LAO TZU
Those who realize that the body is no more substantial than the froth that floats on the waves of the sea, realize that this life is nothing more than a mirage. *- The Dhammapada*	Woe to those ignorant people who desire and grasp after pleasure and things that lead to ruin—those things that lead to suffering and death. *- The Tao Te Ching*
He in whom the self has become extinct is free from lust. He will desire neither worldly nor heavenly pleasures, and the satisfaction of his natural wants will not defile him. *- The Sermon at Benares*	With nothing to drive you, and having no compulsions, needing nothing, being attracted to nothing, then you have gained control and are free. *- Chuang Tzu*
One leaves a smaller joy to attain a greater one. Therefore, leave the small and find that which is great. *- The Dhammapada*	The person who is contented with what they have is richer than the richest. *- The Tao Te Ching*
It is difficult for the man who lives at home and tries to lead a higher life—with its purity and perfection. So let one shave their head and face and dress oneself in the clothing of a mendicant, and go forth and lead a homeless life—forsaking family and property. *- The Tevigga Sutta*	Desire and discontent lead to misfortune. Seeking worldly things is folly. Those who are rich are those who are contented with what they have. *- The Tao Te Ching*

JESUS	KRISHNA
Those who find their life will lose it, and those who lose it for My sake will find it. *- The Gospels of Matthew and Luke* Those who love life will lose it. Those who hate life in this world will preserve it in eternity. *- The Gospel of John*	That person is truly wise who has renounced the world. That person attains the highest good. *- Santiparva Mahabharata*
The disciples of John marry and are given in marriage, but my disciples are like the angels in heaven. *- The Book of John the Evangelist*	Released from lust and anger, the heart controlled, the Self realized, one gains absolute freedom—both here and hereafter. *- The Bagavad Gita*
He that is married should not renounce his wife, and he that is not married should not marry. *- The Gospel of the Egyptians*	Aspiring to God alone, mendicants leave their homes. Knowing this, the people of old did not wish for offspring. *- The Upanishads*
Not everyone can receive this precept, but only those who are ready. There are eunuchs by birth, and there are eunuchs who have been made eunuchs by men, and there are eunuchs who have made themselves eunuchs for the sake of the kingdom of heaven. Anyone who is able to accept this should do so. *- The Gospel of Matthew*	The highest good for one who has mastered his senses and acquired wisdom, is a complete disinterest in the things of the world. *- Santiparva Mahabharata*

BUDDHA	LAO TZU
Make yourself an island. Purge your impurities and you will be free from sin. You will not again see birth and old age. *- The Dhammapada*	I am as fresh as the morning air, pure as a newborn babe, free as a homeless wanderer. Let others lust after wealth. I am content to be nourished by the food of Mother Tao. *- The Tao Te Ching*
The life of a householder is full of hindrances of daily living. It is a path that is defiled by passion. But the one who is free like the air is the one who has renounced all worldly things. *- The Tevigga Sutta*	Where the fountains of passion lie deep, the heavenly springs are soon dry. *- Chang Tzu*
So long as the desire of man towards women, even the smallest, is not destroyed, one's mind is still in bondage. *- The Dhammapada*	The person who is wise does not desire those things which are hard to obtain, nor does he value them. *- The Tao Te Ching*
The man of virtue becomes celibate and refrains from having sexual relationships as householders do. *- The Kevaddha Sutta*	The wise man accedes to the needs of his belly, but not his eyes. *- The Tao Te Ching*

JESUS	KRISHNA
Lust (for pleasures) binds humanity with chains, and holds them in bondage for as long as they seek those things that change and pass away. *- The Book of Thomas the Contender*	The person who is truly wise is the person who has renounced everything having to do with the world. That person attains the highest good. *- Santiparva Mahabharata*
Everyone who seeks truth and wisdom must make wings for themselves in order to fly away from the lust that burns the spirits of humanity. *- The Book of Thomas the Contender*	As a lamp in a windless place does not flicker, so is the yogi who has acquired self discipline. *- The Bagavad Gita*
Matthew said, "How does the small join itself to the Great?" He said, "Let go of all things that cannot follow you." *- The Dialogue of the Savior*	Subduing the body, eating little, with body, speech and mind controlled, he is freed from the notion of "mine." He is fit for becoming God. *- The Bagavad Gita*

BUDDHA	LAO TZU

Desiring future security from bondage one should abandon sensual desire however painful this may be.

- *The Itivuttaka Sutta*

Putting away all thoughts of lust, he lives a life of chastity and purity.

- *The Tevigga Sutta*

Attaining only to the Ineffable, the one whose mind is freed from thought and desire crosses over to the other shore.

- *The Dhammapada*

If our eye of discernment is suddenly opened we will be freed from lust and greed.

- *The Tao Te Ching*

"When wisdom awakens you, you will see truth wherever you look. Truth is all you'll see."

– Ajahn Chah

WISDOM AND KNOWLEDGE

"The foolish reject what they see, not what they think; the wise reject what they think, not what they see…Observe things as they are and don't pay attention to other people."

– Huang-Po

Most of us aren't born with wisdom, although wisdom is latent within us. Knowing this—wishing to become wise—we may go looking for wisdom, but find that it eludes us time and again. We may read hundreds, even thousands, of books—all of the world's sacred scriptures, all of the teachings of all the spiritual masters who have ever lived—and still, wisdom may still escape us.

True wisdom may be gained through living life, and learning from it. But wisdom is ultimately a product of the intuitive mind, not the thinking mind. Gnostic-Christians called the opening of the intuitive mind, "gnosis," or knowledge. Gnosis is not intellectual knowledge, but a deep understanding of how Reality works.

Gnosis, Knowledge, Wisdom—whatever we may choose to call the knowing Self within us—is what happens to us after we exhaust the intellectual mind. Life's "aha!" experiences are flashes of insight that come to us in an instant, without effort. Gnosis happens when our thinking minds are looking the other way. Zen Buddhists refer to such sudden insight as "satori," and Christians might call it "revelation."

Gnostic-Christians spoke of gnosis as "secret" knowledge, yet it is secret only to the extent that most of us don't have spiritual "eyes that see," and "ears that hear." We miss the deep meaning of life due to our craving for material existence. And if we ever transcend our limited perception, gnosis will come in a flash of insight, not from a well thought out paper on philosophy.

If we are unable to see the Kingdom of God, both within us, and all around us, it is only because our perception is focused on the kingdom of Earth. When Jesus was questioned as to whether or not he considered himself a king, he replied that his kingdom was "not of this world."

Many New Testament scholars today like to think of Jesus as a wisdom teacher in the tradition of the Greeks. But Jesus taught the wisdom of God, not of men. In his book, *Meeting Jesus Again for the First Time*, Marcus Borg, a New Testament scholar and professor of religion at Oregon State University, calls Jesus' wisdom, like Lao Tzu's and the Buddha's, "world subverting wisdom." Such deep insight flies in the face of conventional wisdom and encourages people to look at life in entirely new ways. It suggests that happiness may be more important than pleasure, and serenity more important than achieving, acquiring and "being right." Like a Zen master, Jesus used parables and aphorisms to shock people out of their conventional thinking.

The wisdom tradition of Jesus was even more pronounced in Gnostic-Christianity. The word for "wisdom" in the Hebrew Bible, and in Gnostic-Christian texts, is feminine in nature, and when translated into Greek, becomes "Sophia." Gnostic-Christians allegorized Sophia as the divine Mother, and in some texts Sophia was featured as the spiritual consort of the Christ.

Most of us recognize that intellectual knowledge is not the same thing as wisdom, and yet (and I am the greatest of all offenders) we often act as if our intellectual mind will eventually produce profound spiritual awareness. Jesus, the Buddha, Krishna and Lao Tzu tell us that it cannot. The intellect, for all of its merits, is not in charge of perception.

JESUS	KRISHNA
Truth finds those who are virtuous and wise. – *The Dialogue of the Savior*	Out of compassion for them, I abide in their hearts and destroy the darkness born of ignorance, by the luminance lamp of knowledge. – *The Bagavad Gita*
Those who are wise are like the fisherman who caught many fish. He chose the largest fish to keep, and threw the small fish back into the sea. – *The Gospel of Thomas*	The wise, through meditation on the Self, recognizes the Ancient—who is difficult to see—enters the darkness for that which is hidden in a cave, and dwells in the abyss as God. This one leaves joy and sorrow far behind. – *The Upanishads*
How fortunate is the wise man who seeks after truth. When he finds it, no one can disturb his peace. – *The Book of Thomas the Contender*	He who has faith, and who has mastered his senses, attains wisdom. And having attained wisdom, he attains supreme peace. – *The Bagavad Gita*
Understand what is here and now, and you also understand the mysteries. – *The Gospel of Thomas and Kephalaia LXV*	When ignorance is destroyed by knowledge of the Self—that knowledge, like the sun, reveals God. – *The Bagavad Gita*

BUDDHA	LAO TZU
Recognize those things that lead you forward, and those things that hold you back. Choose the way that leads to wisdom. – The Buddha	Perfect wisdom is unplanned. – Chuang Tzu
Those who read many scriptures, but who fail to practice what they contain, are like someone counting someone else's cows. They gain nothing for themselves. – The Dhammapada	A fish trap catches fish, but once the fish is caught, the trap is forgotten... The purpose of words is to convey ideas. But when the ideas are grasped, the words are forgotten. I would like to talk to someone who has forgotten words. – Chuang Tzu
When one transcends inertia through diligent practice, he gains wisdom and his suffering ceases. – The Dhammapada	A wise man is not compelled to leave home and search out grand vistas. He stays home and remains peaceful, above it all. – The Tao Te Ching
The wise man who sees the world as an illusion does not act as if it is real. Therefore he does not suffer. – The Buddha	The wise person sees and hears like a child. He sees what is in front of him, but does not judge or discriminate. – The Tao Te Ching

JESUS	KRISHNA
Everyone who seeks truth through wisdom, escapes those things that destroy the spirits of men. – *The Book of Thomas the Contender*	Those who are wise, understanding the nature of immortality, do not seek for anything among those things that change. – *The Upanishads*
Do not offer to dogs what is sacred, or they will tear you to shreds. Do not throw your pearls before swine, for they will only trample them underfoot. – *The Gospels of Matthew and Thomas*	The wise man should not disturb those of little understanding, who are deluded by the phenomena of the material world. – *The Bagavad Gita*
Be diligent in seeking instruction, and pursue this path with faith, love and good works. Then you will attain to Life. – *The Apocryphon of James*	You have learned the wisdom of the Self, now listen to the wisdom of Yoga so that you may achieve freedom from Karma. – *The Bagavad Gita*
The wise person and the fool cannot live together because the fool has no understanding of life. – *The Book of Thomas the Contender*	Having attained knowledge, one achieves Supreme Peace. Those who are ignorant and without faith, go to destruction, unable to find happiness in this life or in the next. – *The Bagavad Gita*

BUDDHA	LAO TZU
The body is like a delicate piece of pottery. It must be surrounded by the walls of a fortress in order to overcome evil with wisdom. *– The Dhammapada*	It is wisdom to know others; it is enlightenment to know oneself. To conquer others is power; to conquer one's self is strength. *– The Tao Te Ching*
Even though a fool gains the company of a wise man, he does not comprehend Truth any more than a spoon tastes the flavor of the soup. *– The Buddha*	The wise person teaches without speaking. *– Chuang Tzu*
As an irrigator guides water to his fields, as an archer aims an arrow, as a carpenter carves wood, the wise shape their lives. *– The Buddha*	The wise person values those things that others reject, and rejects those things others value. He unlearns his learning and is then able to guide others. *– The Tao Te Ching*
Associating with good people; hearing positive things about people; keeping a right attitude of mind; leading the right life in the Dharma, are all conducive to growth and wisdom. *– The Buddha*	The wise are good at saving others, thus they are not lost. They are good at saving things, so nothing is wasted. This is called following the light within. The good person is the bad person's teacher, and bad persons are the good person's business. *– The Tao Te Ching*

JESUS	KRISHNA
Every one who hears my words and lives by them can be compared to a wise man who built his house on rock. Then the rain fell, and the floods came, and the winds blew and beat upon that house, but it did not fall, because it had been founded on rock. – *The Gospels of Matthew and Luke*	That Yogi who is resolute, who has conquered his senses, and to whom a stone, a piece of earth or a handful of gold are all the same, has gained wisdom and realization. – *The Bagavad Gita*
Arm yourself against the world. Make your defenses strong so that worldly things do not rob you of your birthright. Otherwise, the things you fear will surely take place. – *The Gospel of Thomas*	There are four kinds of virtuous people who worship Me...the distressed, the seeker of knowledge, the seeker of enjoyment, and the wise...of them, the wise, ever-steadfast and fired with devotion to the One, excels. For I am supremely dear to the wise, and that person is dear to Me. – *The Bagavad Gita*
Who, then, is the faithful and wise servant, whom his master has set over his household, to give them their food at the proper time? Blessed is that servant who remains faithful, for the master will set him over all his possessions. – *The Gospels of Matthew and Luke*	At the end of many births, the wise person takes refuge in Me, realizing that all is the Self. This is a very great and rare soul. – *The Bagavad Gita*
Be as wise as serpents and as innocent as doves. – *The Gospels of Thomas, Matthew and Luke*	The wise person bridles his tongue and controls his mind. He keeps his knowledge within himself. – *The Upanishads*

BUDDHA	LAO TZU
As a rock cannot be moved by the wind, those who are wise cannot be moved by praise or blame. *– The Dhammapada*	The heavens last forever, the earth is very old. What is the secret of their longevity? It is because they do not live for themselves. Therefore the wise man becomes last. Denying himself, he is secure. Fulfillment comes to those who are selfless. *– The Tao Te Ching*
Those who lack wisdom are those who have no understanding of the dharma of life. The wise are those whose minds remain balanced and serene. Thus, good and evil do not touch them. *– The Dhammapada*	If excellence comes from non-preference, then the wise person is he who empties hearts of desires. *– The Tao Te Ching*
Those who are immature lose their watchfulness, but the wise guard it as their greatest treasure. *– The Dharmapada*	Once you have fulfilled your purpose, stop there. Do not boast or parade your secret. Give up pride...to over-develop is to increase decline...this is not the Way, and anything that resists the Way will soon cease to be. *– The Tao Te Ching*
The prudent man ministers to the chaste and virtuous. *– The Maha-parinibbana Sutta*	He who speaks does not know. He who knows does not speak. *– The Tao Te Ching*

"Love is a fruit in season
at all times, and within the
reach of every hand."

– Mother Teresa

LOVE AND COMPASSION

"All you need is love."

– *The Beatles*

One of the greatest embodiments of love and compassion in our time is the Dalai Lama. Exiled from his homeland many years ago when the Chinese communists invaded Tibet, the Dalai Lama has nevertheless become an ambassador of love to the entire world—ceaselessly traveling from one land to another, sharing goodwill. When asked what his religion is, he does not begin a long dissertation on the nature of Tibetan Buddhism. Instead, he says simply, "My religion is love." Even though the Chinese government hates and fears him, he refers to them as "My friends, the enemy."

How many of us, having endured what the Dalai Lama has, could respond to such hatred with such love? No doubt, most of us fail to live up to our own expectations when it comes to acting in a loving way. Jesus said that it is easy to love those who love us, and hard to love our enemies—and yet much of the time we find it difficult enough just to love those who love us.

I recall reading a story some years ago about an encounter that took place between a Jewish rabbi and his wife, and a member of a white supremacist group which hated Jews. Circumstances arose in which this young man, along with his brethren, broke into a local synagogue and destroyed much of it, defacing almost every surface with racial slurs and other slogans of intolerance.

If something like this were to happen to most of us, our first reaction might be one of equal anger and disgust. We would call the police with the hopes that the responsible parties would be found, arrested and severely punished. We would probably feel horribly violated, and our intolerance of hate groups would become intense. Some of us might even want to retaliate in kind.

But instead of calling the police, the rabbi and his wife went looking for the responsible people. They were finally able to locate one member of the hate group, and instead of responding to him angrily, they told him that they loved him. This response so disarmed the man, that when the rabbi invited him to dinner at the couple's home, the man actually accepted the invitation.

After dinner, the rabbi and his wife talked with this young man for many hours, during which time he shared his life story with them. It was not surprising for the couple to learn that this poor lost soul had been abused and unloved as a child. Neither was it surprising to them that his role models had been parents who were bigots.

It was apparent to the rabbi and his wife that the young man's hatred had nothing to do with them, any more than it had to do with the fact that they were Jewish. They understood that this young person's hate was really an expression of his own pain and suffering. Life had been hard and cruel to him, so he had become hard and cruel to survive.

The rabbi and his wife did not see a hate-filled criminal before them—someone who ought to be vilified and punished. They saw a human being who was desperately in need of love and compassion. As it turned out, love worked a miracle: not only did the ex-white supremacist voluntarily repair all the damage his group had done to the synagogue, but he became like a son to the rabbi and his wife, and they became the loving parents he never had.

An inspiring true-life story like this allows us to see that love and compassion are more than spiritual platitudes. Hate really can be transformed by love, just as the great spiritual teachers have always told us. To see what we need to do in this world, to recognize the pain and suffering in everyone, we have to transform ourselves into living embodiments of love. If we succeed—through great effort, and many failures—we come to realize that what we did for the sake of others was the very thing we needed to do for ourselves. Love, like hate, returns to the sender.

JESUS	KRISHNA
Love your neighbor as yourself. *The Gospels of Matthew, Mark and Luke*	The true Yogi applies the same standard to others as he applies to himself. Seeing what is pleasure and pain for himself, he knows what is pleasure and pain for others. Thus, he wishes good to all and evil to none. *- The Bagavad Gita*
You have heard it said that, "You should love your neighbor and hate your enemy." But I say to you, Love your enemies and pray for those who persecute you, so that you might be children of your Father who is in heaven. *- The Gospels of Matthew and Luke*	With one's heart centered by Yoga, calm and passive everywhere, the Yogi sees the Self in all beings and all beings in the Self. *- The Bagavad Gita*
For I was hungry and you gave me food, I was thirsty and you gave me drink, I was a stranger and you welcomed me, I was naked and you clothed me, I was sick and you visited me, I was in prison and you came to me...what you did to one of the least of these, my brethren, you did also to me. *- The Gospel of Matthew*	Whatever you do, whatever you eat, whatever you offer in sacrifice, whatever you give away, whatever austerity you practice, do that as an offering to Me. *- The Bagavad Gita*
Love your enemies. Pray for those who persecute you. You will then become children of your Father in heaven. Blessed are the merciful, for they will receive mercy. *- The Gospels of Matthew and Luke*	

BUDDHA	LAO TZU

Being immersed in the highest state of consciousness, the disciple's heart is connected to compassion. He sees himself in all beings, and is free from negative feelings toward others.
— *Doctrinal formulas*

If we sacrifice this body for the world's benefit, then all things will come to that person who loves others as he loves himself.
— *The Tao Te Ching*

With generosity and kind words, always doing to others what is good, he treats all people as the same. His compassion for the world is like the hub that makes the wheel turn round.
— *Anguttara Nikyaya*

Since the sage is in need of nothing, he gives his attention to those who are in need. He is compassionate to the caring and uncaring alike.
— *The Tao Te Ching*

If you do not take care of one another, who else will do so? Those who would care of me, should care for those who are sick.
— *The Buddha*

The world can be turned over to that man who loves all people as he loves himself.
— *The Tao Te Ching*

Everyone fears violence, just as they fear death. Likewise, all people love life. So see yourself in others. Then it is not possible to hurt anyone. Then you can do no harm.
— *The Buddha*

Compassion is what gives me bravery. One cannot become brave without nurturing compassion. Battles are won by compassion. Mercy is victorious. Heaven belongs to those who are merciful.
— *The Tao Te Ching*

JESUS	KRISHNA

It is no benefit to you in loving only those who love you.
Great benefit comes by loving those who hate you.
- The Gospel of the Egyptians

You should rightfully mourn even the downfall of
those who do not believe.
- Agrapha

Your Father...makes His sun rise on the evil and on the good,
and sends rain on the just and on the unjust.
- The Gospels of Matthew and Luke

Be compassionate as your heavenly Father is compassionate.
- The Gospels of Matthew, Mark and Luke

And the righteous answered him, "Lord when did we see you
hungry and fed, or thirsty and give you drink? And when did we
see you a stranger and welcome you, or naked and clothe you?
And when did we see you sick or in prison and visit you? And
the King will answer them, "Truly, I say to you, as you did it to
one of the least of these my brethren, you did it to me."
- The Gospel of Matthew

BUDDHA	LAO TZU
You will only become free by loving those who hate you. *- The Dhammapada*	Do not dismiss those who are evil as unworthy. If you are wise, you will save all men. *- The Tao Te Ching*
Do not mislead anyone, or scorn anyone, anywhere. Never wish for the suffering of others because you are angry or irritated. *- The Buddha*	Were there no weeds, what would gardeners do? *- Chuang Tzu*
With good will for the entire cosmos, cultivate a limitless heart. - Karaniya Metta Sutta	Heaven and earth work together so that the rain may fall equally on all. *- The Tao Te Ching*
Never in this world has hate ever cast out hate. Love alone wins over hate...with this and the knowledge that we will all die, how can you argue with each other? *- The Buddha*	
Just as mother keeps her child from harm, and guards him with her life, so you should treasure all living beings with a grateful heart, spreading love throughout the world. Protect everyone, everywhere, from hatred, and radiate kindness in all directions. *- Doctrinal Formulas*	

JESUS	BUDDHA
When someone wants to take your shirt, let him have your coat as well. If someone forces you to go a mile with him, go with him an extra mile. *- The Gospels of Matthew, Luke and Thomas*	The greatest reward in the world is to provide for others. And there is no greater loss in the world than to accept from others without an attitude of gratefulness. *- The Buddha*
Give to the one who begs from you, and do not turn your back on one who wants to borrow from you. *- The Gospels of Matthew and Luke*	A disciple who seeks well-minded disciples should act without thinking when he performs acts of charity. *- The Dhammapada*
Judas asked, "How should one begin to follow the Way?" Jesus answered, "Love and kindness." *- The Gospel of the Hebrews*	Let one cultivate boundless good will towards the entire world. *- Doctrinal formulas*

JESUS	BUDDHA
Where love does not flow with abundance, all actions are flawed. *- The Manichean Psalter*	One who clings to the Void and neglects compassion, does not reach the highest stage. *- Saraha*
And Jesus went about all the cities and villages, teaching in their synagogues and preaching the gospel of the kingdom, and healing every disease and every infirmity. When he saw the crowds, he had compassion for them, because they were harassed and helpless, like sheep without a shepherd. *- The Gospel of Matthew*	Develop a state of mind of friendliness, for as you do so, ill-will will grow less; and of compassion, for thus vexation will grow less; and of joy, for thus aversion will grow less; and of equanimity, for thus repugnance will grow less. *- Majjhima Niyaka*
I give you a new commandment: Love one another as I have loved you. *- The Gospel of John*	Just as a mother would risk her life to protect her child, so should one cultivate a limitless heart of compassion for all beings. *- The Buddha*

"Men never do evil so completely and cheerfully as when they do it from religious conviction."

– Blaise Pascal

HYPOCRISY

*"Always look at your moccasin tracks first
before you speak of another's faults."*

– *Sauk saying*

The warnings against hypocrisy voiced by Jesus, Buddha, Krishna and Lao Tzu are never directed at the general public. They are directed toward those of us who claim to be religious or spiritual. Their criticisms might sting, but we should be grateful for them. Without recognizing the things we need to work on, we cannot grow.

Puffing ourselves up, being in denial about our shortcomings, not taking responsibility for those times when we injure others by our thoughtlessness—are all attitudes that are self-defeating. Perhaps more than anything else, hypocrisy keeps us bound in the chains of illusion. If we do not practice what we preach, we are not self-aware. And if we are not self-aware, we are not growing.

None of this is news. We all know what hypocrisy is, and some part of us always knows when we are being hypocritical. It is our need to always justify ourselves that keeps us from hearing with open ears and seeing with open eyes. But we never really grow unless our defenses are down. Even our own inner voice can't get through to us unless we allow ourselves to become vulnerable. So, in a way, this chapter is as much about self-awareness as it is about hypocrisy. We can't fix something unless we know it's broken.

There are many similarities between Jesus and the historical Buddha. Their ethical and moral teachings are very similar. They both had life-altering mystical experiences. Both men began movements of religious renewal—Jesus within Judaism, Siddhartha Gautama within Hinduism. But there was one major difference between these two men: Jesus was a social prophet and a social critic, Buddha was not.

If we've had a Christian upbringing, one of the many images of Jesus that might come to mind, is of him giving the religious hypocrites of his day a tongue-lashing. Supposedly, the subjects who bore the brunt of Jesus' challenges were the Pharisees—religious legalists who proclaimed that they were strict followers of the Mosaic Law, the Torah. Jesus accused these legalists of following the letter of the Law, while ignoring its spirit. He criticized them for making a show of their piety, while failing to put their piety into action. Simply put, these legalists didn't practice what they preached. And Jesus pointed this out to them.

But while Jesus is well known for his statements against hypocrisy, the following verses make it clear that he was hardly alone in this. Buddha, Krishna and Lao Tzu were in full agreement with the man from Galilee.

JESUS	KRISHNA
Be careful that your spiritual practice is not in public, so that others know that you are spiritual. When you give to charity, do not announce it like the hypocrites do, so that others may praise them. They already have their reward. Do not let your left hand know what your right hand is doing. Do charity in secret, and your Father will reward you in secret. *- The Gospels of Matthew and Luke*	Those who are filled with self-conceit, who puff themselves up, being proud and drunk from wealth—make their sacrifices in name only, out of ostentation, filled with pride and drunk with wealth, they perform sacrifices to Me in name only. Their pretension, full of ego, lust for power, who are disrespectful and spiteful, hate Me in their own bodies, and in the bodies of others. *- The Bagavad Gita*
Not everyone who says to me "Lord, Lord" will be saved, but only those who do works of righteousness. *- The Gospels of the Egyptians, Matthew and Luke*	Having your mind centered in Me, and through my grace, success will come. But if you practice yoga with self-conceit, you have not understood Me, and you will perish. *- The Bagavad Gita*
Keep away from those who consider themselves to be learned, and like to parade around in their fine vestments, and who love to be noticed and honored in public—those who take the seats of honor in the synagogues, and at feasts. These hypocrites steal from widows even while they say long prayers. The judgment which comes upon them will be great. *—The Gospels of Mark, Matthew and Luke*	Those who do spiritual practices with the hope of gaining respect and honor, performing ascetic practices to gain honor, and who are ostentatious, and who practice austerities with the object of gaining welcome, honor and respect, and with ostentation, are unbalanced, and their actions are fleeting. *- The Bagavad Gita*
Learn to hate that hypocrisy, which is produced by evil intentions. Hypocrisy never comes close to truth. *- The Apocryphon of James*	Those who are motivated by desire and prompted by conceit and insincerity become deluded because of their evil thoughts. That which they produce is contaminated. *- The Bagavad Gita*

BUDDHA	LAO TZU
No monk is a true monk who has not first purified the mind. Those who wear the saffron robes, but lack honesty and self-control are not worthy of wearing the saffron robes. - *The Dhammapada*	Those who make self-conscious displays of spirituality are not sincere, and not in harmony with Tao. Such public display will ultimately ruin the person, since he no longer is protected by Tao. No act not in harmony with Tao can succeed. Every display in public will reap the punishment of men…Be sincere. Be careful not to display yourself. - *Chuang Tzu*
Those who have heard my word but not practiced it, life after life, will descend into the lowest hell. - *The Lotus of the True Law*	When men lost their understanding of Tao, intelligence came along, bringing hypocrisy with it. - *The Tao Te Ching*
Those monks are immature who seek prestige, doing their best to gain influence and admiration…these monks who are puffed up and boastful, insisting on their own point of view, only increase their pride and passion. - *Kevaddha Sutta*	Walking in the Way leads you forward. But you will not achieve recognition by boasting. Arrogance denotes failure. No merit is gained by self-conceit. Leadership is not attained by inflating yourself. - *The Tao Te Ching*
Fools of poor understanding have themselves for their greatest enemies, for they do evil deeds which bear bitter fruit. - *The Dhammapada*	When one ceases to follow Tao, he loses integrity as well. - *The Tao Te Ching*

JESUS	KRISHNA
You blind guides. You strain out the gnat and swallow the camel. *- The Gospel of Matthew*	Fools dwelling in darkness, wise in their own conceit, are puffed up with vain knowledge, go round and round, staggering to and fro, like blind men led by the blind. *- The Upanishads (The House of Death)*
You hypocrites. You are like whitewashed sepulchers, appearing beautiful on the outside, but within are full of dead men's bones and uncleanness. Outwardly you appear righteous before men, but within are full of hypocrisy and iniquity. *- The Gospels of Matthew and Luke*	Those who are enemies of the truth lack morality and understanding. Instead, these damaged souls become enemies of truth, intent upon the destruction of others. Full of hypocrisy, they are deluded and their actions are impure. *- The Bagavad Gita*
They have planted trees without fruit, in my name, in a shameful manner. *- The Gospel of Judas*	Anyone who quieted his body but whose mind is all awhirl restrains the organs of action but meditates with a revolving mind, producing thoughts of objects of the senses, is deluded in understanding, and a hypocrite. *- The Bagavad Gita*
Woe to you, you scholars and Pharisees. You are hypocrites because you keep others from knowing the kingdom of heaven. You refuse to enter, and you will not allow others to enter. *- The Gospels of Matthew, Luke and Thomas*	

BUDDHA	LAO TZU
Those who see sin where there is no sin, and no sin where there is sin—these men follow false teachings and walk the evil path. *- The Dhammapada*	Lack of faith on one's own part encourages faithlessness in others. *- The Tao Te Ching*

The person who tells lies about life goes to hell. The person who does something and says he did not do it, and the person who says he didn't do something, but did—after death these two are equal. These two commit evil deeds even in the next world.
- *The Dhammapada*

They go astray who do not understand the meaning of my words.
- *The Lotus of the True Law*

It doesn't matter how many spiritual books you read. It doesn't matter how many spiritual talks you give. Will it do you any good if you do not act on holy words?
- *The Dhammapada*

JESUS	BUDDHA
Whatever you teach to others with words, be sure to carry out in your actions. *- Agrapha*	Do not pay attention to what others do or do not do. Rather give your attention to what you do, or fail to do. Like flowers full of color but without fragrance are the words of those who do not put into practice what they urge. *- The Dhammapada*
Woe to you, blind scholars and Pharisees—you hypocrites: you clean the outside of the cup and plate, but inside are full of plunder and incontinence. *- The Gospels of Matthew, Luke and Thomas*	Those who follow heretical theories are hard to correct. They have much pride and are hypocritical, twisted, full of malignancies, knowing nothing, and dense. They do not hear the call of the Buddha. *- The Lotus of the True Law*
Why do you see the splinter in someone else's eye, but ignore the log in your own eye. Can you say to others, "Here, let me take that splinter out of your eye," when you do not see the beam in your eye? This is hypocrisy. Remove the log from your own eye so that you can see clearly enough to remove the splinter from your brother's eye. *- The Gospels of Matthew, Luke and Thomas*	Pay attention to your own faults—those things you have done and those you have not. Overlook the faults of others. *- The Dhammapada*
Hear me and understand this: It is not what goes into the mouth that defiles a man. It is what comes out of the mouth that defiles a man. *- The Gospels of Matthew, Mark and Thomas*	Those who are ashamed for what they should not be ashamed of, and unashamed of what they should be ashamed of—such men follow the wrong teachings and take the evil path. *- The Dhammapada*

JESUS	BUDDHA
Though you are in my bosom, but do not do the will of my Father, and do not keep my commandments, I will cast you out saying, "Go away from me, I do not know you." *- The Gospels of the Egyptians, Nazareans, Matthew and Luke*	Even if a monk would take hold of the hem of my robes, and even if he should follow behind me, one foot after another, but who is filled with covetousness and desire, who is spiteful and whose mind is not quieted, such a monk is far from me, and I am from him. *- A Sermon to Monks*
Grapes can not be picked from plants with thorns. Neither is it possible for figs to be picked from plants with thorns. Bad fruit comes from bad trees, good fruit comes from good trees. *- The Gospel of Thomas*	Not consorting with fools, consorting with the wise, paying homage to those worthy of homage: This is the highest protection. *- Mangala Sutta*
Two men went up into the Temple to pray, one a Pharisee and the other a tax collector. The Pharisee stood and prayed thus with himself, "God, I thank thee that I am not like other men, extortioners, unjust, adulterers, or even like this tax collector. I fast twice a week, I give tithes of all that I get." But the tax collector, standing far off, would not even lift up his eyes to heaven, but beat his breast, saying, "God, be merciful to me a sinner!" I tell you, this man went down to his house justified rather than the other. *- The Gospel of Luke*	The foolish person who at least knows he is a fool is wiser than the fool who thinks he is wise. For he is his own worst enemy. The trouble he causes undoes him. Then comes suffering. *- The Dhammapada*

"And could you keep your heart in wonder at the daily miracles of your life, your pain would not seem less wondrous than your joy; And you would accept the seasons of your heart, even as you have always accepted the seasons that pass over fields. And you would watch with serenity through the winters of your grief."

– Kahlil Gibran, The Prophet

SUFFERING

"Pain is inevitable,

suffering is optional."

– *Modern Buddhist wisdom*

Orthodox Christians believe that suffering has meaning, especially the suffering of Jesus. For them, suffering is part of life. It cannot be avoided, and we shouldn't try to avoid it. Instead, we should learn to endure suffering. Suffering teaches us. Suffering tests us. Suffering makes us stronger.

This response to the reality of suffering is well illustrated in the story of Job, in the Biblical book of Job. Job, we are told, was a good and decent man. He was moral and upright in every way. He also had great faith in God.

Job was also blessed with all the good things life has to offer: health, family and wealth. People in Job's circle considered the presence of all these good things to be evidence that if we are just moral and upstanding, and if we have faith in God, God will reward us materially.

But one day, Job's fortunes began to turn. His flocks were slain. His children were killed. And then Job got very sick. He developed sores from head to toe, and was in such misery that he came to curse the day he was born. When Job's friends saw what had happened to him, they said, in effect, "You must have sinned greatly for such calamities to have come upon you." But Job professed his innocence, knowing that he had not sinned.

In misery or not, Job's wife got tired of his whining, and said to him, "Do you still hold fast to your integrity? Curse God, and die." But Job rejected his wife's advice. He maintained his faith in God in spite of all his suffering.

Now the reader knows from the very beginning of this story that everything that befell Job was God's test. Satan (who was not yet a fallen angel) went to God and said, "Sure, Job loves you because he has all the good things of life. But would he remain faithful if you took them all away?" God pondered this awhile, and finally gave Satan permission to put Job to the test.

Even though Job suffered greatly, by the end of the story he has passed every test, so God restored him to health. The moral of the story being that if one's faith in God is true, it does not falter even in the worst of times.

So Judeo-Christianity views suffering as a test of faith and character. The Buddha, however, viewed suffering in an entirely different way. He wasn't interested in the question of whether or not suffering has meaning. He was more interested in finding the cause of suffering, and the way to end it.

The Buddha noted that suffering always arises due to the indulgence of some form of desire. If our house burns down, we are miserable because we desire a house that hasn't burned down. When we get sick, we suffer because we crave health.

For most of us, most of the time, it's hard to remember that pleasure and pain always go hand in hand. We forget that we cannot have one without the other. So we seek to maximize pleasure and do our best to avoid pain. But the great masters knew that life doesn't work that way. Everything in our universe comes to us in pairs of opposites, and the opposites are always changing from one to the other. Pain replaces pleasure, pleasure replaces pain, over and over again, endlessly. Nothing in the material universe ever remains the same for long. But when we finally understand this truth at the most profound level, we have a chance to change the rules of the game.

Buddha taught that there is a way out of suffering, and that way is to eliminate desire. If we can retrain the mind so that it no longer craves, so that it no longer prefers one thing over another—so that good and bad, pleasure and pain, hot and cold, love and hate are all the same to us, then suffering ceases of its own accord.

JESUS	KRISHNA
If you knew how to suffer, you would have the power not to suffer. Know how to suffer, then you will have power not to suffer. *- The Hymn of Jesus from The Acts of John*	Experiences of heat and cold, pleasure and pain are only felt because one's senses are in contact with objects. They come and go. Their nature is impermanent. Endure them with patience. *- The Bagavad Gita*
Blessed are those who are persecuted; they will rest in the light. *- The (Greek) Gospel of Thomas*	The person who remains unmoved in the presence of pleasure and pain is a king among men, and gains the eternal. *- The Bagavad Gita*
I (John) saw his suffering and could not bear it. I turned away and wept. But the Lord stood before me in a vision of light and said, "John, those below us see me as being crucified, pierced, and given bitterness to drink. But hear me—the one who stands before you—and hear what I say…it was not I who was on the cross. *- The Acts of John*	Yoga is a state of severance from the contact of pain. This Yoga should be practiced with perseverance, undisturbed by depression of heart. *- The Bagavad Gita*
My true being is not the body that surrounds me. Therefore, I did not suffer, nor was I in anguish at any time. These people did not harm me. Rather, the rulers of the universe destroyed my body, and it is fitting that they should have done so. *- The (First) Apocalypse of James*	For him whose mind is controlled by meditation, and becomes calm—when the Self is seen by itself, one reaches a state of infinite bliss. When he goes beyond the senses and knows this to be his greatest possession, he rises above the senses, and is undisturbed by sorrow. *- The Bagavad Gita*

BUDDHA	LAO TZU
The wise person who conquers lethargy through practice and sincerity, transcends suffering and reaches the mountain top, which is wisdom. *- The Dhammapada*	I suffer due to my ego and my selfishness. If I became unselfish, how could I suffer? *- The Tao Te Ching*
If the mind is serene at the time of death, some beings rise and attain the heaven-world. *- A Sermon to Monks*	The Self which is under control cannot suffer, but exists forever. *—The Tao Te Ching*

Of those things that come and go, which are affected by suffering, change and decay, one can not say that this is the Self.
- The Buddha

Those who are selfless rejoice in both this world and the next.
- The Dhammapada

JESUS	KRISHNA
This is why you get sick and die: because you love what misleads you. *- The Gospel of Mary (Magdalene)*	For one who is temperate in eating and recreation, in work, in sleep and wakefulness, Yoga becomes the destroyer of misery. *- The Bagavad Gita*

Learn from these teachings, attain Gnosis, love life, then there will be no one to cause you sorrow but you yourself.
- The Apocryphon of James

Do not ask to be released from temptations, for it is through overcoming temptation that you become God's beloved.

Do not fear suffering, for you are protected by a wall of spirit.

The world has existed long before you, and will continue to exist long after you. Your sufferings are but a single hour of a single day.
- The Apocryphon of James

Leave behind you the sufferings and the shame of your flesh. For only when you leave the sufferings and passions of the body behind, will you find enlightenment. Only then will you be One, and reign with the King. For you and He will be one from then on, throughout eternity.
- The Book of Thomas the Contender

BUDDHA	LAO TZU

If you fear suffering, just do no evil deeds…for
all to see, or secretly.
- *The Dhammapada*

Grief and sorrow in the world come to those who hold the
world dear…but happy are they who are free from grief
because they do not hold the world dear.
- *The Doctrine of the Buddha*

With all greed removed, the wise do not see themselves
as higher or lower, or equal to others. They are free from
summoning the cycles of time.

For one who no longer considers anything in the world his own,
and who does not grieve over what is not, who is not influenced
by ideas, that person is said to be at peace.
- *Purabheda Sutta*

There is a place without substance, even beyond the Great
Beyond that I call the end of suffering.
- *The Buddha*

"*What holds on for life so dear this wheel so ceaselessly turning? What wanders back in one more guise, until at last it drops the veil and sees itself within a mirror that holds no reflection?*"

– The Author

KARMA AND REINCARNATION

"The snowdrop is a snowdrop and not an oak, and just that kind of snowdrop, because it is the outcome of the karma of an endless series of past existences."

– *Rhys-Davids*

Karma and reincarnation are topics which cannot be discussed separately since they are inextricably linked. Karma is what *causes* reincarnation, or rebirth. Put an end to karma and you put an end to rebirth.

Karma, literally, means "works" or "actions." Since most of our actions in life have either positive or negative effects on ourselves and others, we can speak of accruing both "good" or "bad" karma during each lifetime. In theory, if our good karma outweighs our bad karma, our next birth will find us in circumstances that are more conducive to spiritual growth. If the opposite is the case…well, we don't even want to think about that.

Karma, we are told, is never neutral. If one becomes enlightened in any given lifetime that person may continue to act, but it is said that no karma of any kind is accrued. Enlightenment frees us from the wages of karma at the same time that it frees us from "samsara"—the ever-turning wheel of birth, death and rebirth.

So who's keeping score? Dualistic religions like Judaism, Christianity and Islam believe the scorekeeper is a supernatural Being who keeps a journal of debits and credits for each person. Eastern philosophies, by contrast, believe that we ourselves are the scorekeepers. But even if there is no supernatural being to pass judgment on us doesn't mean we get a pass. The law of karma suggests that *we* alone are responsible for all of the things that happen to us in this life and the next. Our specific karma is predicated upon everything that we have ever thought, said or done in this life and all those that came before.

Traditional Christians might be surprised to learn that Hindus and Buddhists believe in "heaven" and "hell." But for Hinduism and Buddhism, such positive and negative realms have no location in time and space, and are the product of our own karma. Like all phenomena, heaven and hell are devoid of ultimate reality. Like the life we are experiencing right now, they are projections of our own dualistic and deluded minds.

At least we should be happy to learn that "punishment," the feedback loop of karma and self-judgment, is never eternal. If we reap the negative effects of our actions here, and hereafter, these conditions last only as long as we choose them to. We can begin to alter our karma the moment we decide to leave the world behind and give our full attention and effort to the process of ending our suffering and achieving enlightenment.

Unlike their orthodox brethren, many Gnostic-Christian movements believed in karma and reincarnation, although there are not a great number of references in the recovered texts. Contrary to the opinion of some, there are no references to reincarnation in the canonical Gospels of the New Testament. Certainly the historical Jesus understood the

law of karma (we reap what we sow), but we have no idea what he believed about the afterlife. Many New Testament scholars believe that all of Jesus' references to judgment, the coming apocalypse, heaven, etc. in the canonical Gospels, were not his words, but those of the Christian evangelists who wrote those Gospels.

No doubt there are at least some modern Christians who believe in reincarnation, but don't dare talk about it in church. Certainly this was the case with the early Church. The most famous orthodox Christian who believed in karma and reincarnation was the brilliant third century apologist and theologian, Origen. There is no record that Origen bore the wrath of his brother clerics during his own time, but the Church excommunicated and anathematized him three centuries later just to set the record straight.

Origen cannot have been the only orthodox Christian who believed in the twin doctrines of karma and reincarnation, since these beliefs were specifically repudiated by the Church—not during the third century when Origen lived—but several centuries later. In 553 C.E., the Second Council of Constantinople decreed: "Whosoever shall support the mythical doctrine of the preexistence of the soul and the consequent wonderful opinion of its return, let him be anathema."

While the decree could be considered retroactive, and while it anathematized Origen officially, this could not have been its main purpose. For an anathema against reincarnation to be issued formally suggests that the belief was widespread among Christians even as late as the sixth century.

Reincarnation has always been a difficult doctrine to grasp because there are so many different interpretations about just how it works. The Buddhist understanding of "rebirth," for instance, differs from the Hindu belief in reincarnation. To confuse matters even more, every philosophical system within each of these religions explains the doctrine in a slightly different way—all of which can be confusing to the Westerner who didn't grow up in any of these traditions.

Certainly the Tibetan Buddhists have concentrated on this subject far beyond the scope of other sects or religions. *The Tibetan Book of the Dead* is a guide and road map of what happens between death and rebirth. It is also a good place to begin for those who wish to know more about this subject.

JESUS	KRISHNA
Be merciful that you may obtain mercy; forgive that you may be forgiven. What you do is what will be done to you. As you give, so it will be given to you; as you judge, so you will be judged; as you serve, so will service be done to you; with what you measure out, it will be measured out to you in return. - *Agrapha, and the Gospels of Matthew and Luke*	Everyone is the creator of their own fate, and even their fetal life is affected by the dynamics of the works of their prior existence. - *The Garuda Purana*
Judge not, that you not be judged. For with the judgment you pronounce, you will be judged. - *The Gospels of Matthew and Luke*	What one does in life determines who he is. Those who practice evil become evil. Those who perform acts that are pure, themselves become pure. We are what we do in life. It is our will that determines our fate. - *Brihadaranyaka Upanishad*
Agree with your adversary quickly while you are on the way with him, lest your adversary deliver you to the judge, and the judge deliver you to his officer, and you be cast into prison. Amen, I say unto you, you will not come forth from there until you have paid the last farthing. - *The Gospels of Matthew and Luke*	One who is deluded life after life obtains the wombs of those who are also deluded. Failing to know Me, they fall into ever lower realms of existence. - *The Bagavad Gita*
The soul will be punished...according to transgressions of which it is guilty...then the Virgin of light will bind that soul and hand it over to one of her judges to have it cast into a body which is appropriate for its crimes. - *The Pistis Sophia*	Malicious and cruel evildoers, most degraded of humanity, I hurl perpetually into the wombs of most cruel beings in these worlds. - *The Bagavad Gita*

BUDDHA

As the echo belongs to the sound, and the shadow to the substance, so misery will overtake the evil-doer without fail.
- *Three Sermons*

If you harm one who is innocent, the harm comes back to you like dust thrown into the wind.
- *The Dhammapada*

If an evil person criticizes someone who is virtuous, it is like spitting at the sky. The spit doesn't dirty the sky, but returns to pollute the person who spits.
- *Three Sermons*

Misfortune will be the end of those who practice little virtue. They will be tormented in the six worlds.
- *The Lotus of the True Law*

JESUS	KRISHNA
Let the sheep not fear the wolves after death, nor fear those who can kill them. Rather, they should fear those who have power over body and soul, and are able to cast them into the fires of hell. *- The Gospel of the Egyptians*	There are two eternal paths: one light, the other dark. The first leads to liberation from the wheel of death and rebirth. The other path leads to this world again. *- The Bagavad Gita*
Forgive us our debts as we forgive our debtors. *- The Gospel of Matthew*	As blazing fire reduces wood to ashes, so does the fire of knowledge reduce all Karma to ashes. *- The Bagavad Gita*
Strive now to gain the mysteries of the Light—that the sufferings of this life may end, and you may enter the Light-kingdom. Do not wait, day after day, or one life after another, thinking you will gain the mysteries after you have come into another body. *- The Pistis Sophia*	If one does not attain God before death in this life, he must again take the body of a mortal. *- Katha Upanishad*
The rulers (of fate) give the old soul a cup of forgetfulness, and the old soul will drink of this cup and forget all the regions to which it has gone, and all the punishments through which it has traveled. And the cup of forgetfulness becomes the body which surrounds the soul. And it resembles the soul in all of its shapes, and makes itself like it. This is a false spirit. *- The Pistis Sophia*	Many are the births that have been passed through by Me and you. I know them all, while you do not. *- The Bagavad Gita*

BUDDHA

Those who seek happiness by inflicting pain on
others—who are also seeking happiness—will
not find happiness after death.
- *The Buddha*

Everything that we are is the result of our former thoughts
and actions. If we speak evil, or act with evil intention, then
suffering follows us. If we speak and act with good intentions,
happiness will follow us like a shadow.
- *The Buddha*

Refrain from doing evil, for suffering follows this path. But
suffering cannot touch one who does good. Make yourself a
fortress both within and without, so that nothing can assail
you. Time is short. Not even a minute of it should be wasted.
- *The Dhammapada*

Pleasures flow everywhere. You float upon
them and are carried from life to life. Like a hunted hare you
run, the pursuer of desire pursued, harried from life to life.
The cycle of birth and death is a long path for those
who do not know the dharma.
- *The Dhammapada*

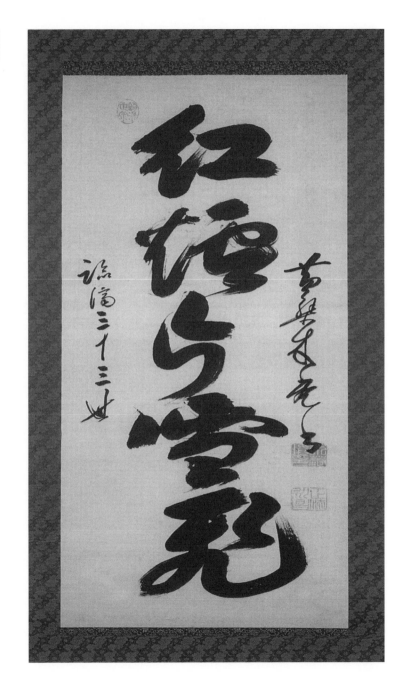

JESUS

(For the disembodied soul that has become perfected),
Let the Virgin of Light cast him into a body which will
be righteous and good, so that it flies high and
inherits the kingdom of Light.
- *The Pistis Sophia*

KRISHNA

The Yogi who strives diligently, and is purified
of defilements, and who gains perfection through
many births, then achieves the highest goal.
- *The Bagavad Gita*

BUDDHA

Of those taking on rebirth, those who have done evil go to a place of great suffering. Those who have done good go to a place of joy. But those with a pure heart enter Nirvana.

– *The Dhammapada*

"There is no death.

Only a change of worlds."

— Chief Seattle

DEATH AND
IMMORTALITY

"For what is it to die but to stand naked in the wind and to melt into the sun? And what is it to cease breathing, but to free the breath from its restless tides, that it may rise and expand and seek God unencumbered?"

– *Kahlil Gibran*, The Prophet

Of all animal species on Earth, only Homo sapiens know they will die. Knowing this, all human beings have to face the fear of dying. It seems almost unimaginable that "I" will cease to exist. It seems ludicrous that our *experience* of reality will end in utter annihilation. Certainly total extinction has to be the most frightening thing we can imagine.

The ancients sought a remedy for the fear of dying, and developed religions to deal with the fear. Most of the ancient religions suggested that we don't really die, but live on in one form or another after our physical body goes back to the earth from which it came. Even though they wished to give their followers hope, how did these first religionists *know* what happened after death? Did they commit suicide so they could come back to life and explain what death was like? Or did they simply tell people to believe and have faith that their doctrines about death and the afterlife were accurate?

The problem is that everyone talks about death (if they dare mention it at all) from *this* side of the grave. Do any of us speak from experience? One of my favorite stories illustrating this question is about a Zen monk who asked his Zen master, "Roshi, is there life after death?" The Roshi answered, "I don't know." The monk was incredulous at this answer, and blurted out, "But Roshi, you're a Zen master!" To which the Roshi replied, "Well yes, but I'm not a *dead* Zen master!"

Tibetan Buddhists, on the other hand, claim to know a great deal about death and the process of dying—even the process of rebirth. *The Tibetan Book of the Dead* is purported to be a primer and navigational chart relating to what happens to us after death. It discusses what takes place as the body is dying, and the "bardo" planes of existence that we go through after we are dead. Tibetan Lamas even claim to remember their past incarnations—which can be confusing to the non-Buddhist because Buddhists do not believe in a human soul. If there is no soul, what is it, then, that leaves the body at death? What is it that experiences the "lokas," or other worlds (or planes of existence) including heavenly and hellish realms, not to mention demons and deities? More puzzling still, what is it that is reborn? If "I" no longer exist, who or what takes on a new body? *What* has existed through countless incarnations? *What* can break the bonds of samsara and attain Nirvana?

Christians believe each one of us has a soul, but the belief that the soul flies off to heaven or hell immediately after death is actually a Christian heresy. The "true" Church doctrine holds that our souls do not separate from our bodies, but both body and soul remain together in the ground until the day of judgment—at which time all good Christians will rise from their graves in reconstituted bodies (with souls intact) and ascend into heaven, where they will live in God's presence for all eternity. But woe to all those dead who died without having confessed Jesus Christ as their Lord and Savior; these unfortunate pagans will also rise from their graves, but only to be sent directly to hell where they will be tortured for all eternity.

Another group of people with strong convictions about the after-life are those who draw conclusions from the "near death" experiences of others. People such as Dr. Raymond Moody have documented many cases of people who claim to have experienced after-death states where they find themselves floating above their bodies while doctors are trying to revive them. More than a few of these people tell of being drawn toward a brilliant light at the end of a long dark tunnel where they may meet long dead relatives, or even find themselves in the presence of a divine being such as Jesus or the Buddha.

Modern science, on the other hand, denies that near-death experiences have anything to do with life after death. They point out that people who had these experiences did not, in fact, die, and almost dying is not the same thing as being dead. Explaining the near-death experience, researchers argue that the brain secretes certain chemicals as the body is shutting down, and these chemicals cause the dying person to have pleasant hallucinations. But when these hallucinations dim, researchers tell us, all brain activity ceases, and consciousness comes to an end.

Those scientists who do work on the human brain go further yet in telling us that none of their electronic instruments have ever measured any form of energy leaving the body at the time of death. As far as they are concerned, science has proven once and for all that there is no such thing as a human soul. In this, they agree with the Buddha: "When the body and mind dissolve, they do not exist anywhere, any more than musical notes lay heaped up anywhere."

Yet while Buddhists deny the existence of the human soul, they believe that there is some form of consciousness that experiences phenomena after death. And they also believe in "rebirth." But what is reborn? The Buddhist answer is that there are "samskaras," or collections of karmic tendencies and patterns that are attached to "us" during this lifetime. This core, or "mind-stream," because it still craves material existence, perceives phenomena after death in the same way it perceived phenomena while in a physical body. But

because of the craving for material existence, these "mind-streams" are eventually drawn back into the material realm.

On the subject of death, there is one extremely important teaching that seems to be common to all four of the spiritual teachers in this book. Jesus, the Buddha, Krishna and Lao Tzu make the point over and over again that the fear of death is the worst possible state of mind a person can be in at the moment of death. The fear of death, it would seem, affects what we perceive after we die. If we are fearless at the moment of death, we see death for what it is: just another illusion. In this case, we do not "taste" death. But for those with fear, the after-death state can be a nightmare.

Interestingly, this is precisely what those who have had near-death experiences tell us. For them, the fear of death no longer exists. Knowing this, they are able to live life more fully in the here and now.

Certainly the Buddhist and Hindu would agree. If there is no immortality in the usual sense of the term, neither is there "death." If nothing is born, nothing dies. Perhaps it is in this recognition that we come to realize that the fear of death is an inappropriate, and unnecessary, response to the dissolution of the human body.

JESUS	KRISHNA
When what animates a person is removed, that person is called dead, and when what is alive leaves what is dead, that which is alive will be summoned. *- Dialog of the Savior*	Of that which is born, death is certain; of that which is dead, birth is certain. One should not grieve over the unavoidable. *- The Bagavad Gita.*
Every nature that takes on form exists in and with all other forms. Each will return to its own original form and nature. *- The Gospel of Mary (Magdalene)*	All beings are unmanifested in their beginning, manifested in their middle state, and unmanifest again in their end. What is there to grieve about? *- The Bagavad Gita*
Do not run from death, but seek it out. For when you look at death closely you will discover within it your salvation. For no one who fears death will be saved from it. Scorn death and take thought of Life! *- The Apocryphon of James*	It is not that we have never existed, or that we will cease to exist in the future. As childhood becomes youth and turns to old age in this body, the embodied soul will find another body after death. Souls that are calm souls are not deceived by the threat of death. *- The Bagavad Gita*
The souls of every human generation will die. When these people, however, have completed the time of the kingdom and the spirit leaves them, their bodies will die but their souls will be alive, and they will be taken up. *- The Gospel of Judas*	The world is the wheel of God. All living creatures revolve on its rim. The world is the river of God, with all streams coming back to Him. On the great wheel of being goes the individual self. Around and around, believing itself to be separate from all else. Until at last it sees itself as God and attains immortality. *- The Shvetashvatara Upanishad*

BUDDHA	LAO TZU
Not in the sky, nor in the midst of the ocean, nor deep in the mountain, nowhere can you hide from your own death. *- The Dhammapada*	A living person is soft and flexible, but upon dying becomes stiff and rigid. Thus the soft belongs to the living, and the hard to the dead. *- The Tao Te Ching*
	To be heavenly is to be one with the Tao; to be one with the Tao is to abide forever. This one is safe even after the body dissolves. *- Tao Te Ching*
Death is not to be feared so much by one who has lived wisely. *- The Buddha*	Those of old did not dread death because they had no lust for life. They came into the world without gladness, and left it without resistance. Their coming was easy. So was their going. *- Chuang Tzu*
Those who understand the teachings of the dharma transcend death...Death takes those who pursue pleasure, but those with wisdom go beyond. *- The Dhammapada*	All things come together in One. Life and death are equal. *- Chuang Tzu*

JESUS	KRISHNA
Judas asked, "Does the human spirit die?" Jesus answered, "This is why the creator ordered Michael to give the spirits of people to them on loan, so that they might serve. But the Great One ordered Gabriel to grant spirits of the great generation (of enlightened beings), which has no ruler above it—the spirit and the soul. Therefore the souls will find rest." *- The Gospel of Judas*	The embodied one having gone beyond the three natures, out of which the body is evolved, is freed from birth, death, decay, and pain, and attains to immortality. *- The Bagavad Gita*
Jesus said, "I am now going back to that place from which I have come. If you wish, you can come with Me." His disciples said to him, "If you tell us to, we will come with you." But Jesus answered, "No one will ever enter the kingdom of heaven because I told them to—but only those of you who have perfected themselves." *- The Apocryphon of John*	At the end of life, leaving the body, that person attains to the object of his attention. So, constantly remember Me...with mind and intellect absorbed in Me, you will surely come to Me. *- The Bagavad Gita*
His disciples said to him, "On what day will rest come to those who are dead, and on what day will the new world come?" He said to them, "The rest that you wait for has already come, and you have not recognized it." *- The Gospel of Thomas*	The unreal never is, and the Real never is not. Those who understand this have found truth. Everything that is pervaded in this way is certain to be indestructible. No one has the power to destroy the Absolute. *- The Bagavad Gita*
Whoever seeks to save his life will lose it, and whoever loses his life will preserve it. *- The Gospels of Luke, Mark, Matthew, and John*	Anyone who thinks the Self is the slayer and the slain does not understand. *- The Bagavad Gita*

BUDDHA	LAO TZU
The master found his disciple crying, and said, "For whom do you cry? For whom are you sorry. If you are weeping because I do not know where I am going, then you are mistaken. If I did not know where I was going, I would not leave you. Your tears are because you do not know where I'm going. If you did, you would not be weeping. The essence of Dharma knows no birth, no death, no coming or going." *- The Manual of Zen Discipline*	For one who has found peace in life cannot be touched by the weapons of war. The buffalo finds no place in him to place its horns. The tiger finds no place to sink its claws. Thus, there is no room for death in such a person. *- The Tao Te Ching*
If you are vigilant you can go beyond death. If you lack such powers of vigilance you cannot escape death…meditating with vigilance, the wise come to life. *- The Dhammapada*	Those who do not have the means to live do not fear death. Thus they are greater than those who make too much of life. *- The Tao Te Ching*
The sage knows the beginning and the end of consciousness, its production and passing away. The sage knows that it came from nowhere and returns to nowhere, and is empty of reality, like a conjuring trick. *- The Buddha*	
Death carries off a man who is gathering flowers, and whose mind is distracted, as a flood carries off a sleeping village. *- The Dharmapada*	

JESUS	KRISHNA
The disciples asked him, "Tell us about our end." Jesus said, "You ask about your end, but have you even discovered your beginning? He who knows the beginning knows the end, and will not experience death. *- The Gospel of Thomas*	Those who understand the Self as indestructible, changeless, without birth, and immutable, can neither slay or be slain. *- The Bagavad Gita*
There are five trees that exist in Paradise. They do not change with the seasons, and their leaves do not fall. Whoever experiences these, will not experience death. *- The Gospel of Thomas*	The indwelling Self is changeless, but these bodies have an end. *- The Bagavad Gita*
The heavens and the earth will open in your presence. And the one who lives in Him will not see death. He who becomes One is greater than the world. *- The Gospel of Thomas*	He sees who sees the Lord Supreme existing equally in all beings, sees the deathless in the dying. *- The Bagavad Gita*
Blessed is he who existed before he came into being. *- The Gospel of Thomas*	Whoever meditates on Me alone at the time of death will go forth, leaving the body, and attain to My Being. There is no doubt about this. *- The Bagavad Gita*

BUDDHA

He who knows that this body is without substance, like a mirage, will never meet Mara, the king of death.
- *The Dharmapada*

Remembering that the body is froth, a mirage, you will defeat the temptations of Mara. Death will never again touch you.
- *The Dhammapada*

When the body and mind dissolve, they do not exist anywhere, any more than musical notes lay heaped up anywhere. All the elements of being come into existence after having been non-existent; and having come into existence, pass away.
- *The Visuddhimagga*

When a person dies, he lets go of thoughts about what is "mine". The wise have already done so.
- *The Jara Sutta*

JESUS

Anyone who understands these words will
never experience death.
- *The Gospel of Thomas*

Those who receive life and believe in the
kingdom will never leave it.
- *The Apocryphon of James*

KRISHNA

Those who strive for freedom from old age and death,
taking refuge in Me—they know God, and realize the
ultimate Reality, and Karma in its entirety...continue
to know Me at the time of death, steadfast in mind.
- *The Bagavad Gita*

The Self is said to be unmanifested, unthinkable and
unchangeable. Knowing this, one should not mourn.
- *The Bagavad Gita*

BUDDHA

LAO TZU

Having awakened from a dream, one forgets those
whom he encountered therein. So it is with those
who die. They do not remember those people
whom they treasured in life.
- *The Jara Sutta*

Wakefulness is the way to life. The fool sleeps
as if he were already dead, but the master is
awake, and he lives forever.
- *The Buddha*

"Having shed your skin
completely, one true reality
exists. It shines throughout
all time, with no distinction
of measure or time."

– Keizan

ENLIGHTENMENT AND LIBERATION

"I have only one purpose: to make man free, to urge him towards freedom; to help him to break away from all limitations, for that alone will give him eternal happiness, will give him the unconditional realization of Self."

– J. Krishnamurti

The true mystic—the one who has finally, totally and completely let go of the world—has but a single goal: to be united with the Source of his or her spiritual yearning. This Source of Being that draws each of us at our own speed has been called many things, and gone by many names. It has been spoken of, always imperfectly, by countless seekers—each trying to find the map that will show the Way home.

Jesus, Krishna, the Buddha and Lao Tzu tell us that the Way, the map that points the direction back home, lies within ourselves. But they also correct our misperception that there is a destination. They insist that there is no map, no home, no pilgrimage, nothing to do, nowhere to go, nothing to achieve, and nobody to become. They tell us that we are already home; that we are already One; that we already live in the Kingdom of God. To see this for ourselves, we have only to drop the gossamer veil that separates us from our Beloved.

Like the human need for religion, the yearning to be reunited with the Ground of Being, the desire to take the Way that leads back "home," seems to be rooted in human consciousness, perhaps even encoded in our DNA. And yet, yearning alone is not enough. Jesus, Buddha, Krishna and Lao Tzu tell us that we will not achieve enlightenment, or attain liberation merely by hoping for it. While they can light the way, they can't take our journey for us.

As we near the end of this book, the reader may have realized, as I have, that it is not about many different things, but just one: freedom. And what is freedom but to be released from the shackles of our own making? The teachers whose words are recorded here offer us the greatest treasure in the world: freedom from the limitations of perception, freedom from the cares of the world, freedom from attachment, freedom from craving, freedom from doubt, freedom from karma, freedom from suffering and freedom from fear.

In the end, though, all the words in this book are just words. They provide a window, not a door. The great spiritual beings of all ages tell us the same thing: "We can unlock your cage. We can open the door. But it is up to you to come out and fly away home."

JESUS	KRISHNA
I have overcome the world. Do not let the world overcome you. I have become free of the world. You too become free of it. *- The Gospel of the Savior*	Released from lust and anger, the heart controlled, the Self realized, absolute freedom is for such sannyasis here, both here and hereafter. *- The Bagavad Gita*
Everyone who has heard and learned from the Father, comes to Me. *- The Gospel of John*	He who works for Me alone and has Me for his goal, is devoted to Me, is freed from attachment, and bears enmity towards no creature. He enters into Me. *- The Bagavad Gita*
When all the trials of life are ended, and one awakens, he sees nothing like it was before. Such a path is attained by those who have ended ignorance, letting it go as if it was nothing more than a dream. No longer do they value those things of the material world. They leave ignorance behind like sleep. *- The Gospel of Truth*	Those who abandon all religion and take refuge in Me, the Self, the Lord of Illusion, will cross over the Illusion to Me. *- The Bagavad Gita*
Because you have renounced all, and have endured all sufferings, and because of your rebirth from one body to the next, you have become pure light. You will ascend and be king of the kingdom of Light. *- The Pistis Sophia*	The all-knowing ruler of all, as minute as an atom, which upholds all, and whose form cannot be known, but shines like the sun, beyond the illusion—those who meditate on Him with devotion, and with an unwavering mind...at the time of death, reach Him. *- The Bagavad Gita*

BUDDHA	LAO TZU
The wise, his fetters burst, the urge for further life exhausted, no more the prospect of rebirth for him at death, but full release. *- The Sanskrit Dharmapada*	When nothing drives or compels you, when needs are ended and there is nothing to attract you, then everything is in its place. You are free. *- Chuang Tzu*
He will go to the other shore and stand on dry land if he has realized liberation and hidden knowledge in this life. *- Catukka Nipata Pali*	Knowing that which does not change is enlightenment, not knowing it is blindness...to be one with Tao is divine. Though you may die, you will not perish. *- The Tao Te Ching*
If the eye never sleeps, all dreams will naturally cease. If the mind makes no discriminations, the ten thousand things are of a single essence. *- The Buddha*	The mind of one who has wisdom and serenity becomes the mirror of the Universe and the eyepiece of all creation. *- Chuang Tzu*
The heroic sage who has broken every bond, has achieved peace, rid of all defilements, this one is enlightened, no longer troubled with doubts, and has arrived at the end of action, released from clinging that brings destruction. *- The Itivuttaka sutta*	Can you purify your mystic vision and wash it until it is spotless? *- The Tao Te Ching*

JESUS	KRISHNA
Whoever has true knowledge of God, ascends to the Father, and abides in Him who has neither beginning or end. *- The Sophia of Jesus Christ*	Offering all actions to the Lord, with the chains of bondage broken, and with a heart unwavering in the Yoga of renunciation, he is liberated, and comes to Me. *- The Bagavad Gita*
When you cast away the blindness of ignorance, you will have left this prison of flesh and reached Him-who-is. No longer will you be James, but the One-who-is. *- The (First) Apocalypse of James*	Those who have achieved perfection and reached Me, will not be born again into this body which is changeable and full of pain. *- The Bagavad Gita*
Now let all rejoice. Seek the Light, that the power of the stars which is in you, may live. *- The Pistis Sophia*	Those freed from attachment, fear and anger, and trusting in Me, attains My Being. *- The Bagavad Gita*
That which has held me in this prison has been conquered, ignorance has died, desire ended—The cycles of forgetfulness are no more. Free at last, I will receive my rest within the silence of Eternity. *- The Gospel of Mary (Magdalene)*	All of the worlds...are subject to return, but after attaining Me, there is no rebirth. *- The Bagavad Gita*

BUDDHA	LAO TZU

One who is a master of knowledge, who has lived a holy life, has gone to the end of the world and reached the distant shore.
- *The Itivuttaka Sutta*

In the absence of passion he becomes free, and when he is free, he becomes aware that he is free; and he knows that rebirth is exhausted, that he has lived the holy life, that he has done what behooved him to do, and that he is no more for this world.
- *The Fire Sermon*

Free from appetite and craving, rejoicing in freedom, the sage becomes a light in this world. Pure, shining, free.
- *The Dhammapada*

I have traveled through many rounds of birth and death and birth again, looking for the maker of this house, but I found him not. Now, at last, I see you, house-builder. You shall not build this house again, for its beams are torn apart, its rafters broken. With desires ended, I have attained to the Eternal.
- *The Dhammapada*

SOURCES AND TRANSLATIONS

The Parallel Sayings is a book that I have wanted to write ever since I recognized the connection between Gnostic Christianity and Eastern philosophy—three decades ago. But taking on such a project seemed daunting to me. Simply teasing out the parallel sayings from literally hundreds of ancient texts would, I knew, require a great deal of time. Dealing with multiple translations of texts would be yet another challenge. Still, I began collecting and categorizing sayings five years ago, with the hope that I could one day assemble them into a book like this.

Another challenge I faced, and perhaps the reason no one else has yet attempted a project like this before, is the reality that most all English translations of texts written in other languages are under the copyright of translators and publishers. While it is possible to receive permission from a publisher to use a small number of quotations in a scholarly work, most publishers will not grant permission to use their translations for a book like *Parallel Sayings* because they view such works as competition. The only recourse is for the author to do all the translating him or herself.

While I can still stumble my way through ancient Greek—the language the *New Testament* was written in, I do not know Coptic (the Gnostic Gospels) or Sanskrit (Hindu texts) or Pali (just one of the many languages in which Buddhist texts were written) so doing my own translations were out of the question.

Even if copyright issues were not a problem, there would still be the question of what translation of a text to use. Translations vary widely, and can be quite dissimilar from one another. The fact is that many translators take great liberties with a text, and do not even attempt to translate word for word—which can be frustrating to a scholar.

I think translators will also admit that something is always lost in translation, no matter if it is translated word for word, or not. Languages never translate exactly from one to another. In *New Testament* scholarship it is very important to be able to read the original text in Greek. Let me give you a couple of examples why understanding the original language makes a difference.

At the end of *The Gospel According to John* (21:15-17), the resurrected Jesus asks his disciple, Peter, if he loves him.

Peter says, "of course I love you." Then Jesus asks the question a second time, and Peter gives the same response. Then Jesus asks the question a *third* time, and Peter gives the same response yet again.

This passage won't make much sense to someone who just reads the English translation. The reader is likely to think that Jesus is being obtuse by asking Peter the same question over and over again. But while the passage makes little sense in English, it makes perfect sense in the original Greek.

The ancient Greeks had thirty-three different words for the single English word, "love," which tells us that the Greek language was full of nuance. Almost everyone is familiar with one of these words: "eros," meaning sexual love. The Greek *New Testament* used two other words for love: "agape," which means unconditional spiritual love, and "philia," which refers to the kind of love friends share.

Armed with this knowledge, we can now read the Greek text of *John* in a new light. Jesus asks Peter if he loves ("agape") him, but Peter answers using the word "philo." Jesus is asking for Peter's unconditional spiritual love, but Peter answers by saying, "Yes, I have *affection* for you." Jesus gives Peter a second chance to make good by asking the question again. But once again Peter fails to live up to Jesus' expectations. The third time Jesus asks Peter if he loves him, Jesus uses the word, "philia," instead of "agape," signifying that he finally accepts Peter's limitations.

A more important example is *Luke* 17:20, where Jesus says that the kingdom of God is not something one can find by physically looking for it. Rather, the kingdom of God is *entos*, "within you." The Greek word, "entos," can be translated as either "among you" or "within you," but most Christian translators render the word "among you." Yet the New Testament scholar, C. H. Dodd, demonstrated many years ago that "entos" used in this particular context can *only* be translated as "within you."

Orthodox Christian theology has always insisted that the "kingdom of God" is something that will come in the future, at the end of time. But Jesus in *Luke* is clearly saying just the opposite. The kingdom is not *coming*, nor can it be observed, because it is already here! It exists in the heart of every human being. The version of this saying in *The Gospel of Thomas* has Jesus go one step further by stating, "The kingdom is within you *and* all around you." *Thomas'* Jesus believes that those with spiritual eyes are able to recognize the kingdom as being everywhere.

Ultimately I decided that the only way I could bring this book to fruition was to consult as many translations of a text as I could find, and then use none of them. Instead, I chose to reword them, but only after taking great pains to be absolutely faithful to the meaning of the saying, and using wording that does not change the meaning. In the case of the Gnostic and Apocryphal Gospels, following this process has also allowed me to illuminate otherwise cryptic sayings of Jesus that would be confusing to the reader in their original form.

CHRISTIAN / GNOSTIC CHRISTIAN SOURCES

The Gospel According to Thomas

The Gospel According to Thomas is attributed to the disciple Thomas—or more accurately, Judas Thomas, who in this work is identified as the "twin" brother of Jesus: "These are the secret words that the living Jesus spoke and Didymus Judas Thomas wrote down." Didymus in Greek means "twin", as does Thomas in Aramaic. But Judas Thomas must be understood as the spiritual, not physical, twin of Jesus.

Of all the ancient Christian texts which have been (re)discovered over the past two centuries, *The Gospel According to Thomas* is by far the most important. What makes *Thomas* stand out above all other works is the fact that it contains a number of formerly "lost" sayings of the *historical* Jesus which are not found in any of the canonical Gospels. Secondly, *Thomas* contains sayings of Jesus that have parallels in the canonical Gospels, but the Thomasian versions of these sayings have been shown to be the more original versions.

Three fragments from *The Gospel of Thomas*—written in Greek—were discovered at Oxyrhynchus, Egypt, during the nineteenth century. But the entire text of *Thomas*—written in Coptic—was discovered at Nag Hammadi, Egypt, in 1945—and is part of the famous *Nag Hammadi Library*. The Oxyrhynchus papyruses have been dated to the third century C. E., while the Nag Hammadi papyrus dates to the fifth century. The original text of *Thomas*, however, was written during the first century C. E.

Thomas' 114 logia, or *sayings* of Jesus, were compiled in two stages. The first layer of *Thomas* was written around 50 C. E., making it one of the earliest known compilations of Jesus' teachings. A second, and clearly Gnostic, layer was added to *Thomas* sometime around the end of the first century. The *Gospel* is attributed to the disciple, Thomas, but like all early gospels, was composed anonymously.

The Book of Thomas the Contender

Also discovered at Nag Hammadi, *The Book of Thomas the Contender* (or "spiritual athlete") is a revelation dialogue between the Christ—in a "revealed," non-physical, form—and his "twin," Judas Thomas. This document, along with *The Gospel of Thomas* and *The Acts of Thomas*, can be attributed to a Thomasian tradition which was primarily Gnostic-Christian. The work was probably composed sometime during the second half of the second century.

The Gospel According to Mary (Magdalene)

The only Gospel attributed to a female disciple of Jesus, *The Gospel of Mary* was discovered in 1896—in the possession of an Egyptian antiquities dealer, and is part of a compilation of texts known as Codex Berolinensis 8502, or the *Berlin Codex*. This codex also contained three other works: *The Act of Peter, The Apocryphon of John*, and *The Sophia* (Wisdom) *of Jesus Christ*.

The Gospel of Mary is thought to have been produced in final form around 125 C. E., and is particularly important because it provides evidence of a struggle between matriarchal and patriarchal apostolic traditions in the early Church. Mary Magdalene's right to speak in Jesus' name in this text is challenged by Simon Peter and his brother, Andrew, who together represent the patriarchal viewpoint of orthodox Christianity.

The Church, founded on the patriarchal traditions of Peter and Paul, found it necessary to suppress the tradition of Mary Magdalene, and deny her—and all women—the right to preach and teach in the Church. Ten pages of *The Gospel According to Mary*—roughly half of the original work—are still missing.

The Acts of John

Even though it was considered heretical by the orthodox Church, *The Acts of John* has been handed down from ancient times through copying and recopying. *Acts* has some connection to Johannine literature in general, and may not have been in written before the third or fourth century. Many scholars, however, believe that the Hymn of Jesus—known also as the Round Dance of the Cross, and by other names— was part of a very early Christian ritual.

The Apocryphon of John

A copy of the *Secret Book of John* was discovered at Nag Hammadi, but two other versions of John are also extant. This work, most likely written during the second half of

the second century is clearly a Gnostic-Christian text, and has little relationship with other works attributed to the disciple, John.

The Book of John the Evangelist

Unknown prior to the twelve century, this text was probably written prior to the fourth century since it is clearly a Gnostic-Christian treatise that attributes creation to Satan, rather than to the Hebrew God, Yahweh. Its theology about the Christ is also docetic: Jesus was not human, but was of heavenly origin.

The Kerygmata Petrou

The *Kerygmata Petrou*, or "teachings of Peter," are actually part of a much larger work known as the *Pseudo-Clementines* (works "falsely" attributed to Clement of Rome, the early second century bishop of the Catholic Church.) The *Pseudo-Clementines* have not come down through history in their original form, but derive from a basic document thought to have been written during the middle of the third century. The text of the *Kerygmata*, like much of the *Pseudo-Clementines*, is largely Gnostic in origin, yet goes back to the core of Jewish-Christianity. Among other elements, it includes a very revealing polemic against the self-proclaimed apostle, Paul.

The Gospel According to Philip

The Gospel of Philip was discovered at Nag Hammadi and is not a gospel in any true sense of the term. It contains only a few sayings attributed to Jesus, and is otherwise a theological exposition of the Valentinian school of Gnostic-Christianity. It was written as late as the second half of the third century.

The Apocalypse of Peter

The Apocalypse of Peter is another text that was discovered at Nag Hammadi, and was also written during the third century. It is a revelation dialogue between the "living" Jesus and Peter. The Apocalypse deals at some length with the persecution of Jesus, and the Gnostic-Christian under-standing of his suffering. The anonymous author accuses the Church of being the true persecutor of the living Jesus.

The Apocryphon of James

The Apocryphon, or *Secret Book of James,* was discovered at Nag Hammadi in 1945. It takes the form of oral instructions given to Jesus' brother, James, and to Simon Peter, by the risen Christ during the 550 days that preceded his ascension. Probably written during the early part of the second century, *Secret James* shows Gnostic elements, but includes other early Christian material as well.

The (First) and (Second) Apocalypses of James

As with the *Apocryphon of James*, this text is attributed to James the Just. James was a Nazarite priest, the physical brother of Jesus, and leader of the early Jesus movement. Here, however, it is James' spiritual kinship with Jesus that

is stressed. Both the first and second Apocalypses attributed to James were discovered at Nag Hammadi, thus both texts have Gnostic tendencies, while at the same time showing the influence of Jewish-Christianity. Both Apocalypses attributed to James complement one another in stressing different aspects of the James tradition.

The Gospel of the Hebrews; The Gospel of the Nazoreans and The Gospel of the Ebionites

These three Gospels no longer exist, even in fragmentary form. They are known only through the testimony of early Church fathers who quoted from them. The names of the Gospels in those writings are often interchangeable, but scholars have determined that the quotes come from three different Gospels. Because the Church patriarchs who quoted from these lost texts were the enemies of the Christians who used them, we cannot be sure that their quotes are accurate.

Each of these lost Gospels—like the canonicals—were narrative in style, and were probably written sometime during the first century. Jewish-Christianity, the earliest form of this faith, was eventually condemned as heresy by the orthodox Church.

The Didache (Teaching of the Twelve Apostles)

Mentioned in the writings of Clement of Alexandria, a single manuscript of *The Didache*, dated 1056, was discovered in 1873. The text itself was probably written during the second half of the first century. *The Didache* is an instruction manual for converts of an early Jewish-Christian community.

Dialogue of the Savior

The single extant manuscript of *Dialogue* was discovered at Nag Hammadi in 1945. The dialogue is between the risen Christ and several of his disciples. *Dialogue* was probably composed during the first half of the second century, although parts of it may be earlier. Generally considered a "Gnostic" Gospel, *Dialogue* shares some similarities and comparisons with the *Gospel of Thomas*, the canonical Gospels of *John* and *Matthew*, and *The Apocryphon of James*.

The Gospel of Eve

The only Gospel under the name of an Old Testament figure, this lost Gospel of Gnostic character is mentioned only in the writings of Epiphanius, and the quote which appears in this work is the only known reference.

The Gospel of the Savior

This formerly lost Gospel was discovered in 1967 among the possessions of a Dutch antiquities dealer, and now resides in the Berlin Egyptian Museum. After many years of study by scholars, the text was published in 1997. The remains of this Gospel are extremely fragmentary, but enough of the text remains for scholars to be able to state that it is probably of Gnostic-Christian origin. While no date of composition has yet been determined, the manuscript was probably written no later than the beginning of the fourth century C. E.

The Epistula Apostolorum

Discovered in Cairo in 1895, and composed during the middle of the second century, the *Letter of the Apostles* is addressed to churches of "the four regions of the world." Its content is primarily orthodox—even anti-Gnostic at times—but still contains some Gnostic motifs. The *Epistula* can be credited to a form of Hellenized Egyptian Jewish Christianity.

The (Living) Gospel of Mani, The Manichean Psalms (Coptic Psalm Book), and The Book of Mysteries

These three works come from the third century school of Manichaeism founded by the prophet, Mani, and Mani himself may have written both the Gospel attributed to him, as well as *The Book of Mysteries*. A Persian mystic, the "arch-heretic" Mani fused Buddhism, Zoroastrianism and elements of Christianity to establish a new religion that was so popular, and so widespread, that it rivaled Catholic Christianity. Manichaeism may be considered a major world religion, having existed in the East for centuries after it was suppressed in the West by the Church of Rome.

The Sophia (Wisdom) of Jesus Christ

Manuscripts of *The Sophia* were discovered both as part of the Berlin Codex, and again as part of *The Nag Hammadi Library*.

A Gnostic revelation dialogue between the risen Christ and several of his disciples, the *Sophia* is a Christian reworking of a pagan text known as *Eugnostos the Blessed*, and may have been written as early as the second half of the first century.

The Pistis Sophia (Faith Wisdom)

A very lengthy revelation dialogue, the *Pistis Sophia* (Codex Askewianus) was discovered in a London bookstore in 1773. It consists of four sections or books. One section of the work is dated to the first half of the third century, while the other sections were composed later.

The Two Books of Jeu

As part of *Codex Brucianus (Bruce Codex)*, *The Two Books of Jeu* (Jesus) was rediscovered in 1769, in Thebes, Egypt. It has much in common with *Codex Askewianus* and is mentioned twice in the *Pistis Sophia*. Composed during the first half of the third century, this work is another Gnostic-Christian revelation dialogue between the "living" Jesus and his disciples.

The Book of the Great Logos According to the Mystery

This title is the general heading for the manuscripts within the *Bruce Codex*—which contain *The Two Books of Jeu*.

The Gospel of Truth

A product of Valentinian Gnosticism, *The Gospel of Truth* was discovered at Nag Hammadi in 1945, and was referenced by the orthodox heresiologist, Irenaeus, in his *Adversus Haereses*. Composed during the middle of the second century, this work may have been written by Valentinus himself.

The Naassene Psalm of the Soul

The Naassenes were an early Gnostic-Christian "heretical" sect which the Church attacked through the writings of Irenaeus and Hippolytus. These heresiologists quoted from Naassene texts which are no longer extant. Our single quote comes from the writings of Hippolytus.

Mandaean Liturgy—from the Ginza

The Mandaeans, also known as Sabians, were generally thought to have founded their Gnostic sect prior to the formation of Christianity. Adherents claimed to be disciples of John the Baptist, and the sect itself has survived to the present day in Iran.

The Second Treatise of the Great Seth

Another revelation dialogue, this Gnostic-Christian work was discovered at Nag Hammadi. Purporting to give the true history of Jesus, and concentrating on his torture and crucifixion, this text maintains the docetic nature of Jesus' appearance on Earth.

The Tripartite Tractate

From Codex I of *The Nag Hammadi Library*, this tractate is a text from the Valentinian school of Gnosticism, and was probably written sometime during the early part of the third century C.E. Rather than promoting the usual Valentinian Godhead composed of a masculine/feminine dyad, this text argues for a monadic first principle.

The Thunder: Perfect Mind

This unique document from *The Nag Hammadi Library* (but one that cannot be called Gnostic), was most likely used as a hymn. Its first person style is feminine in nature. "Thunder" (feminine) *is* Perfect Mind, which suggests that the divine extends into the world. Thunder's self-proclamation is in the "I am" style, and the verses are often antithetical or paradoxical. As such, it bears a close similarity to the "Hymn of Christ" from the Acts of John, parts of the Mandaean *Ginza*, the *Gospel of Eve*, and portions of the Hindu *Atharva-Veda*, *Svetasvatara Upanishad*, and *Bhagavad Gita*.

The Trimorphic Protennoia

Also found at Nag Hammadi, this text is also written in the feminine person, and also uses "I am" statements. The *Trimorphic Protennoia* ("first thought") consists of the Light that descends into darkness, the speech of Thought and the Word or Logos of the Thought, which descends to earth and assumes human appearance. In its descriptions of the descent of the Logos, the text bears a striking resemblance to Johannine literature: namely *The Gospel of*

John and *The Apocryphon of John*. The first part of this text was not originally Christian, but underwent several stages of development. The last, and most Christian, revision was written no later than the middle of the second century.

The Gospel of the Egyptians

The apocryphal *Gospel of the Egyptians* is an altogether different work from *The Gospel of the Egyptians*, which is part of *The Nag Hammadi Library*. Almost nothing of it remains other than quotations found in Clement of Alexandria's work, *Stromateis III*. A number of early Church fathers mentioned this Gospel in their writings. Origen knew of it, Hippolytus wrote that it was used by the heretical Naassenes, and Epiphanius mentions that the Sabellians used it as well. *The Gospel of the Egyptians* was probably written during the first half of the second century.

GENERAL SOURCE TEXTS AND COLLECTIONS

New Testament Apocrypha, Volumes I & II, Wilhelm Schneemelcher, Editor, Revised Edition, Louisville, Westminster / John Knox Press, 1997.

The Apocryphal New Testament, M. R. James, Editor, London, Oxford University Press, 1976.

The Nag Hammadi Library, James M. Robinson, Editor, Revised edition, San Francisco, HarperSanFrancisco, 1990.

The Pistis Sophia—a Gnostic Gospel, G.R.S. Mead, Editor, USA, Garber, Communications, 1984.

The Didache, Ancient Christian Writers, New York, Paulist Press, 1948.

Gospel of the Savior, Charles W. Hedrick, Paul A. Mirecki, Sonoma, Polebridge Press, 1999.

The Complete Gospels, Robert J. Miller, Editor, Sonoma, Polebridge Press, 1994.

FOR FURTHER STUDY

Doresse, Jean, *The Secret Books of the Egyptian Gnostics*, New York, MJF Books, 1986.

Jonas, Hans, *The Gnostic Religion*, Boston, Beacon Hill, 1958.

King, Karen, *What Is Gnosticism?* Cambridge, Harvard University Press, 2003.

Koester, Helmut, *Ancient Christian Gospels*, Harrisburg, Trinity Press International, 1990.

Mead, G.R.S., *Fragments of a Faith Forgotten*, London, Theological Publishing Society, 1906.

Pagels, Elaine, *The Gnostic Gospels*, New York, Random House, 1979.

DID JESUS
TRAVEL TO TIBET?

"Those of us committed to promoting a better grasp of the historical Jesus question today usually find ourselves busy with the misconceptions of traditionally religious people, but we must not avoid the very different, and equally dubious, accounts of Jesus popular in less traditional quarters."

– *Robert Price, Professor of Scriptural Studies
at Johnnie Colemon Theological Seminar*

I'm often asked about the story of St. Issa, the nineteenth century legend about Jesus traveling to Tibet to study with the Buddhist lamas there. Even though this legend was proven a hoax during its own day, New Agers have resuscitated it and insist that it is real history. The legend itself is fraudulent, but I can understand why people would want to believe it (or a similar one which has Jesus living in India). There are aspects of Jesus' teachings that make many people feel that he must have received an education in Eastern philosophy. And if it could be shown that Jesus' teachings were essentially the same as those of Krishna in Hinduism, and the Buddha in Buddhism, then one could make a legitimate argument that the Church has misrepresented Jesus for two thousand years.

But similar teachings do not necessarily suggest direct influence. Certainly the current New Age belief that Jesus traveled to Tibet to study with Tibetan lamas has no basis in fact. Buddhism didn't even arrive in Tibet until the seventh century!

Much of the speculation that Jesus traveled outside of his homeland has been based on a misconception about Gospel "history." People read Luke's story about Jesus appearing in the Temple at Jerusalem when he was twelve years old, and then wonder what he did from that age until the time he began to teach around the age of thirty. What happened to these "lost years" of Jesus?

Many readers are not aware that *New Testament* scholars long ago discounted Luke's story as a Christian myth, not history—as are most of the stories about Jesus in the Gospels. So Jesus' "lost years" are really *all* of the years of his life. Scholars concluded more than a century ago that the historical Jesus is buried under so many layers of Christian myth, that we can know next to nothing about him as a historical person.

Virtually all reputable New Testament scholars recognize that the nativity stories and genealogies of Jesus are the myths of later Christians (like those who wrote *Matthew and Luke* around the end of the first century, C.E.) who wanted to tie Jesus to Israel's Messianic tradition that began with King David. New Age authors who claim that Jesus was married and had children who carried on his "royal blood line," are unaware that their new myths about Jesus are founded on very old myths.

The bottom line is simply this: real historians know nothing at all about Jesus' life prior to the beginning of his ministry, and very little about him afterward. He appeared on the stage of history for no more than a year, and then he was crucified. If we speculate that he may have traveled to India or Tibet, then we might as well speculate that he traveled to Siberia or the Americas to study with shamans.

In my opinion, no such conjectures are necessary to explain Jesus' teachings. If Jesus was an enlightened being like the Buddha, then his wisdom came from the vary same Source. Jesus took the road less traveled: the road *within*.

The Hoax of Saint Issa

The nineteenth century Saint Issa ("Issa" means "Jesus" in Arabic) hoax features a cast of very interesting characters. Playing the lead role is one Nicholas Notovitch, Russian Jew, Greek Orthodox convert, war correspondent, spy, bon vivant and the author of *The Unknown Life of Jesus Christ*.

The book, published in 1894, was supposedly based on a two-volume manuscript Notovitch discovered at the Tibetan lamasery of Hemis in 1887, titled *The Life of Saint Issa*. Touring Tibet on horseback, Notovitch claimed that he fell from his horse one day and broke his leg, whereupon he was carried to the local lamasery to recover. It was here where he was shown the amazing Issa material.

Playing the role of foil to Notovitch, was the great Orientalist, Max Muller, editor of the famous *Sacred Books of the East* series. Muller, having read Notovitch's book, wrote to him and stated that, if the manuscripts he discovered were real, they would have been included in the Tibetan canon: The *Kanjur* and *Tanjure*—which, of course, they were not.

Muller also informed Notovitch that an unnamed English woman had sent him a letter stating that she had traveled to Leh in Ladakh, had gone to the lamasery to check out Notovitch's story, and was told by the abbot there that no such document existed. According to the letter, the abbot further stated that there was not a word of truth to

Notovitch's story, that no Russian had ever come there, and that there was certainly no record of any Issa, Jesus or Christ, in any Tibetan literature.

Reeling from Muller's attack, Notovitch changed his story. In the preface to the 1895 edition of his book, Notovitch then claimed that he had written his book based on information gleaned from numerous fragments of many different Tibetan scrolls. There was no longer any mention of a two-volume manuscript.

This same year, Professor J. Archibald Douglas of Agra traveled to the Tibetan lamasery to interview the abbot as well. The abbot—who had been abbot there for fifteen years, and a monk for forty-two years—was outraged by Notovitch's claim. He called St. Issa a hoax, and told Professor Douglas that Notovitch had never been to the lamasery, and there was so such manuscript.

For all intents and purposes, Nicholas Notovitch's book, *The Unknown Life of Jesus Christ* (in Tibet) was discredited, and the whole legend passed out of the public's consciousness—at least for awhile. But for a Hindu swami or a Buddhist lama teaching in the West during the early part of the 20th century, the thought that Jesus may have been part of their religious heritage was tantalizing. To have proof that Jesus studied in the East would further validate Eastern philosophy, while encouraging dissatisfied Christians to convert to Hinduism or Buddhism.

In 1922, Swami Abhedananda—a disciple of the great Vedanta sage and mystic, Ramakrishna, traveled to Hemis with the intention of discovering the truth of Notovitch's claims for himself. Supposedly, a lama showed the swami a manuscript like the one Nicholas Notovitch claimed to have seen. The swami wrote a book titled Journey into *Kashmir and Tibet*, in which he claimed that this was the case.

It's right about here where the historical record gets fuzzy. According to one account, Abhedananda translated the document himself. In another account, someone translated it for him. But no swami and no lama has even been able to produce a text for anyone else to examine. The abbot of Hemis, himself, denied the existence of any manuscripts about Jesus. Abhedananda's disciple, Prajnananda, admitted years later that when he went to the monastery and asked to see the manuscripts, he was told that the scrolls had disappeared!

In 1925, one Nicholas Roerich, a theosophist mystic and painter, visited Ladakh and supposedly heard tales about Saint Issa. But when Roerich quoted the texts he later claimed to have seen at the monastery at Hemis, his quotes were either identical to Notovitch's words, or came straight out of the book *The Aquarian Gospel of Jesus Christ*—a "channeled" work written by Levi Dowling in 1908.

Notovitch's book was reprinted in 1926, and this stirred things up anew. A year later, Edgar J. Goodspeed wrote a book entitled *Strange New Gospels*, subsequently expanded into two books: *Modern Apocrypha and Famous "Biblical" Hoaxes*. Goodspeed described in his books just how Notovitch's hoax had been created, and that seemed to end matters for a second time.

But you can't keep a good hoax down! In 1939, Dr. Elisabeth Caspari, who claimed to belong to a Mazdaznan (an invented modern reincarnation of Zoroastrianism) sect, made yet another pilgrimage to the Hemis monastery. She and her companions later claimed that the lamas themselves presented her with books that revealed that Jesus had been there. But, of course, no one in her party could read the documents, so they really had no idea at all what they had seen.

Lacking any real evidence—an actual manuscript (or even photographs of it) that could be documented and studied—the image of a Tibetan Jesus still became holy dogma of first, the Theosophical Society; and second, the offshoot Summit University—aka Summit Lighthouse, aka The Church Universal and Triumphant, aka The Mighty I Am Movement, aka the cult of Elizabeth Claire Prophet.

And so it is with Saint Issa, the imaginary Tibetan Jesus who managed to study with Buddhist lamas seven hundred years before there *were* Buddhist lamas. But lack of evidence and proof for something one really wants to believe doesn't stop many people from believing a myth. Even though there is not a shred of evidence that a St. Issa ever existed, the myth has become fact for many. Among New Age groups that have wholly accepted Notovitch's hoax as historical truth are Paramahansa Yogananda's Self Realization Fellowship, the Sathya Sai Baba movement, the Hare Krishnas, and The Church Universal and Triumphant.

Certainly I can understand why all of these groups would like St. Issa to have been real, and why they might wish for a Tibetan Jesus. But is it really necessary to manufacture hoaxes in order to connect Jesus with Hinduism and Buddhism? Aren't his teachings (including those in the Gnostic Gospels) enough to show that Jesus' spiritual philosophy had much in common with Hinduism and Buddhism? Orthodox Christians, of course, would argue against such a premise, but after having studied Jesus'

teachings all my life, I believe that there are more similarities than differences.

When I was in college in San Francisco many years ago, I took a course on *The Bagavad Gita* from a professor who was a Caucasian woman, and who was also a follower of the Vedanta school of Indian philosophy. On one occasion our class took a field trip to the local Vedanta temple. In complete silence, we students filed in and took our seats, the incense encouraging an attitude of reverence.

As I looked around, I saw something that surprised me: a large panel containing a row of bronze images of what I took to be great Indian saints. But there amongst them was one image that looked just like most people's conception of Jesus! When I asked my professor about this after the service, she replied, "Oh yes, Vedanta considers Jesus to be one of the world's great spiritual masters." Indeed, Hinduism believes that Jesus was an avatar. Apparently Jesus didn't have to travel to India or Tibet to receive this honor. He just had to be Jesus.

(A special thanks to Robert M. Price, Jesus Seminar Fellow, and Professor of Biblical Criticism for the Center of Inquiry Institute, for compiling the above information on the St. Issa hoax—first printed in "The Fourth R," a quarterly journal of the Westar Institute, Polebridge Press, Santa Rosa, California, May – June, 2001.)

ABOUT THE AUTHOR

"As a man whose own spiritual intensity has taken him from renegade Lutheran pastor to the no-brand seeker of truth he is today, Hooper can certainly irritate your comfort zones. One sometimes imagines that if James Dean, minus the cigarette, had been thoroughly educated in the great religions and a whole lot smarter, he might have been Richard Hooper."

- Larry Moffitt, Editor, United Press International
ReligionandSpirituality.com

Disc Productions, an independent record label specializing in world music and environmental sound.

For the past thirty-five years Mr. Hooper has kept current with academia's "quest for the historical Jesus," and his research in the area of Gnostic Christianity and its relationship to eastern philosophy. Mr. Hooper is also a featured weekly columnist for United Press International's ReligionandSpirituality.com.

Richard Hooper received his Bachelor of Arts degree in the philosophy of world religions from San Francisco State University in 1966, and his Master of Divinity degree from Pacific Lutheran Theological Seminary in 1970. He was ordained by the American Lutheran Church in 1971 and served as the Church's authority and spokesperson on the Church and Counter Culture, in addition to founding a ministry for youth culture on the Monterey Peninsula of California.

In 1978 Mr. Hooper left the ministry and entered the world of business, first as a radio commentator on religious issues, and then as a nature recordist and founder of World

Also available by Richard Hooper:

– *The Crucifixion of Mary Magdalene:*
The Historical Tradition of the First Apostle,
and the Church's Campaign to Suppress It

– *The Gospel of the Unknown Jesus:*
The Secret Teachings of Jesus from the
Apocryphal and Gnostic Gospels

For further information, books and articles by Mr. Hooper, visit our website at SanctuaryPublications.com. Also read Richard's spiritual commentaries each week at ReligionandSpirituality.com.

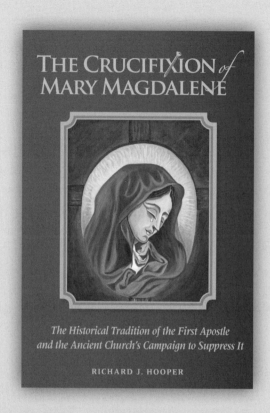

THE CRUCIFIXION of MARY MAGDALENE

*The Historical Tradition of the First Apostle
and the Ancient Church's Campaign to Suppress It*

RICHARD J. HOOPER

For further information, please contact:

Sanctuary Publications
P. O. Box 20697 ■ Sedona, AZ 86341
info@SanctuaryPublications.com

From the earliest days of Christianity, Mary Magdalene has been the subject of controversy, rumor and innuendo. Yet the historical Mary was neither a prostitute nor the wife of Jesus. The canonical Gospels are clear that Mary was Jesus' most faithful disciple. She remained to witness his crucifixion after all of the male disciples had fled in fear. Shortly after Jesus died, she had a powerful experience of the living Jesus and, as a consequence, became the first apostle of Christianity. The Gnostic Gospels further claim that Mary was a leader, teacher, visionary, and—because of her holiness—Jesus' most beloved disciple.

And yet the early Church felt threatened by Mary Magdalene to such an extent that it found it necessary to obscure her real importance, alter her historical tradition, suppress the theology she became associated with, and ultimately discredit her by reinventing her as a wanton woman.

Through a careful examination of more than twenty ancient texts in which Mary Magdalene appears, the author—a former Lutheran pastor—lays bare orthodox Christianity's age-old conspiracy against Mary, and reveals her true role as the primary founder of Christian faith.

350 pages ■ $19.95
ISBN 0974699543 ■ 9780974699554

THE GOSPEL OF THE UNKNOWN JESUS

THE SECRET TEACHINGS OF JESUS
FROM THE APOCRYPHAL
AND GNOSTIC GOSPELS

EDITED AND WITH INTRODUCTION BY
RICHARD J. HOOPER

From the place of Light I go forth.
I come to feel the hearts, to measure
and try all minds, to see in whose heart
I dwell—in whose mind I repose. Who
thinks of Me, of him I think. Who calls
my name, his name I call. Who prays
my prayer from down below, his prayer
I pray from the place of Light.

– Mandaean liturgy

D uring the fourth and fifth centuries of the Common Era—in an attempt to wipe out heresy—hundreds of early Christian texts were destroyed by order of the Roman emperor, Constantine, and the bishops of the Church of Rome.

Thought to have been lost for all time, many of these "heretical" gospels, epistles, apocalypses and apocryphons have been re-discovered during modern times. Other non-canonical texts survived history in whole, or in fragmentary form, and became part of the New Testament Apocrypha. Fragments of still other lost works survived in the form of quotations found in the writings of the early Church fathers.

Now for the first time ever, the most profound and eloquent of Jesus' lost teachings from thirty-four of these texts (as well as many isolated sayings attributed to him) have been brought together in a single volume. In mystical language reminiscent of Krishna in the Bagavad Gita, The Gospel of the Unknown Jesus brings a unique and timely message for all humanity.

The world is a bridge. Cross over it,
do not install yourself upon it.
– Agrapha

Sanctuary Publications
$16.95